The Hymns & Orisons of Lord Shiva
[SHIV CHALISA]

DIAMOND POCKET BOOKS
SELECTED BOOKS FOR ALL

GENERAL BOOKS

Title	Author	Price
Remedial Vaastushastra	Dr. Bhojraj Dwivedi	200.00
Comprehensive Vaastushastra	Pt. Gopal Sharma	60.00
Sampuran Vaastushastra	Dr. Bhojraj Dwivedi	150.00
Commercial Vaastu	Dr. Bhojraj Dwivedi	200.00
Environmental Vaastu	Dr. Bhojraj Dwivedi	150.00
Practical Vaastushastra	Acharaya Satyanand	150.00
Study of Omens	Dr. Bhojraj Dwivedi	60.00
Truth of Life	Veena Malik	40.00
General Knowledge Today (1999)	Sanjeev Arora	40.00
The Book of Best Quotations	Dr. B. R. Kishore	30.00
Nostradamus & Prophecies of the Next Millenium	A. K. Sharma	150.00
Tabassum's Jokes *(Translated by)*	B. K. Chaturvedi	35.00
India : A Travel Guide	Dr. B. R. Kishore	250.00
Cheiro's Language of The Hand	Cheiro	40.00
Cheiro's Book of Astrology	Cheiro	50.00
Cheiro's Book of Numberology	Cheiro	30.00
Learn Hindi in 30 days	Krishna Gopal Vipal	30.00
Hindi Learning & Speaking Course	Krishna Gopal Vipal	20.00
Eve in the India Kitchen	Manjal Kishore	20.00
Famous Tourist Centres of India	B. K. Chaturvedi	60.00
Charle's Crosswords Book	P. Charles	25.00
Dances of India	Dr. B. R. Kishore	25.00
Dresses & Costumes of India	B. K. Chaturvedi	20.00
Yoga-The Light of Spiritual Discipline	Acharya Bhagwan Dev	20.00
Jewellery of India	B. K. Chaturvedi	20.00
Diamond's Book of Word Power	P. Charles	20.00
Diamond's Dictionary of Synonyms	P. Charles	40.00
Ecstasy & Agony	Dr. Giriraj Shah	30.00
In the Shadows of Taj (Novel)	Amitra Sahaya	40.00
Freedom Struggle of India	R. N. Sanyal	30.00
Home Decoration	Dr. Renu Gupta	60.00
The Dictionary of Antonyms	P. Charles	25.00
Indian Microwave Cooking	Tehlina Kaul	100.00
Hypnotism	Acharya Vipul Rao	50.00
543 Faces of India (Hard Bound)	H.D.Singh	1500.00
543 Faces of India (Paperback)	H.D.Singh	1000.00
Laughing Jokes	G.C.Goel (Editor)	40.00
Naughty Jokes	G.C.Goel (Editor)	40.00
Society Jokes	G.C.Goel (Editor)	40.00
Children Jokes	G.C.Goel (Editor)	40.00
Delighting Jokes	G.C.Goel (Editor)	40.00
Thrilling Jokes	G. C. Goel (Editor)	40.00
Hilarious Jokes	G. C. Goel (Editor)	40.00
Computer Hardware Repairing Guide	Shashank Johri	50.00
Computer Programming & Operating Guide	Shashank Johri	40.00
Diamond's Vocabulary Test	P. Charles	25.00
Mathematical Puzzle	B. K. Chaturvedi	25.00
Love Letters for you	B. K. Chaturvedi	30.00
Dyamic Business Letter Writer	Dr. B. R. Kishore	30.00
Everyday Letters	Dr. B. R. Kishore	35.00
Numerology	Dr. B. R. Kishore	20.00
Rafi Ke Nagme (Roman)	Dr. B. R. Kishore	50.00
Chess for Pleasure	Dr. B. R. Kishore	25.00
Chanakya Neeti	B.K. Chaturvedi	40.00
Kautilya Arthshastra	B.K. Chaturvedi	40.00
Clinton Lewinsky Scandal	Ashok Kumar Sharma	60,00
Jyotish & Santan Yog	Dr. Bhojraj Dwivedi	75.00
Sensational Sachin	Lokesh Thani	60.00
English-English Hindi Dictionary	Dr. Baljit Singh & Dr. Giriraj Sharan Agarwal	150.00

SONGS

Title		Price
Songs of Rafi		30.00
Hit Songs of Lata		30.00
Hit Songs of Kishore		30.00
Hit Songs of Mukesh		30.00

Diamond Pocket Books (P) Ltd. X-30, Okhla Industrial Area, Phase-II, New Delhi-110020

The Hymns & Orisons of Lord Shankar
[Shiv Chalisa]

B.K. Chaturvedi

Diamond Pocket Books Pvt. Ltd.,
X-30, Okhla Industrial Area, Phase-2
New Delhi–110020

The Hymns & Orisons of Lord Shiv
(Shiv Chalisa)

ISBN 81-7182-169-3

© *Publisher*

Publisher   :   **Diamond Pocket Books (Pvt.) Ltd**
                            X-30, Okhla Industrial Area, Phase-II
                            New Delhi - 110020
                            Ph.: 6841033, 6822803, 6822804
                            Fax : 011-6925020
                            ~~erms~~@nde.vsnl.net.in
                            ~~~~ondpocketbooks.com

Composed at   :   Printexcel, 30-B, Ber Sarai,
                        Opp. J.N.U., Ph.: 6853397

Preface

Lord Shiv has been the most adored deity among all the gods of Hindu Pantheism. There is hardly a city of town or village in India which doesn't have a Shiv-Mandir or Shivalaya. It is because he is a deity of feeling. To worship Shiv what is required is genuine devotion and not the ceremonial rituals, etc., which are necessary to worship Lord Vishnu. Despite his such great popularity with devout masses and lots of hymns and orisons scattered in the scriptures, there is no collection of these available in one book. It is our attempt to eke out this lacunae by means of this tiny book, which contains all the renowned hymns, orisons, Stutis, Aartis, etc., plus the prominent scriptural details of this Grand God. For the convenience of our devout Shiv- Bhaktas not versed in Nagari script, we have rendered the translations in English and Hindi alongwith the original text also in the Roman script with appropriate diacritical notations. All the necessary mythological references have also been explained in the beginning for the better comprehension of various prayers, etc., which have been sung in hundreds of temples of Lord Shiv all over the world, for many millenia. It is hoped that our devout Shiv-Bhaktas all over the world will acord his this tiny book a 'devoted' welcome.

B.K. Chaturvedi

Contents

I. Lord Shiv: A Deity Extraordinary

Lord Shiv is a unique god in the entire godheads of the Hindu belief. He is incomparable with any other god. He dresses differently; his manners, living style, his dwelling places—all are different. But he is one of the members of the all-pervading Trinity, and a very powerful one. For only he has the power to alter even the rule of Destiny. He is 'moody', inhibition-free, easy to please, protector of those whom no one cares to protect. There are scores of attributes of this Grand Deity or Mahadeva which distinguish him from other gods, But his these very qualities made him supremely adorable god. His is actually a multifaceted personality. Till Rigveda, Shiv's only Rudra from has been mentioned. Then after other, benevolent aspects began to join his personality. He became, Lord Chandrashekhar, Mahadev, Tripurari and the description of his belongings and dresses also underwent a slight change. Ravan's Shivstrota make him wear the elephant's skin which became tiger's in later descriptions. Since he is described as the sole deity responsible for destruction, he came to be associated with various destructive Goddesses like Durga and Kali who were actually the fiery, masscring forms of Goddess Parvati. He is the only deity who, while operating on the mortal plane is described to have married twice, once with Sati, the daughter of Daksha and after her death by self immolation, with Gauri (Uma or Parvati), the daughter of the Mountains. His different aspects of personality appear to have surfaced by the need of time. This led many to believe that Lord Shankar was originally an 'Unaryan Devta' who was brought in the Aryan fold after many centuries. As Mahadeva, he is worshipped by various gods including Brahma and Vishnu. He is Mahakaal, destroys and dissolves everything into nothingness, but he as Shankara, also resorts and reproduces that which has been destroyed and dissolved. His symbol of phallus symbolises this reproductive power. As a Mahayogi, the great ascetic, he combines in himself the highest perfection of austere penance and abstract mediation. In this form he is a naked ascetic or Digambar, that is, clothed with the sky or space. He is also called Chandrashekhar (the moon-crested); Gangadhara (bearer of Ganga), Girisha (the Mount-Lord); Mahakaal (TIME); Pashupati (Lord of Beasts), Vishwanath (Lord of the Universe) and in many more ways. In fact, it is difficult to summarise his all attributes in this kind of book. Suffice it to describe this deity of contradictions by resorting to an old Sanskrit verse, which is quoted below:—

भीर्तिनैव पुंग भुगवविषात् प्रीति न चन्द्रमृतात्
ना शौचं हि कपालमाललुलनात् शौचं न गंगाजलात् ।
नो द्वेग: चिति भस्म नो न च सुखम गौरी स्तनालिंगनात्
आत्माराम तया समाहित हित: स्वस्थ: हरषै: पातु वह ।।

Meaning : He is one who is neither fearful of the deadly serpents coiling round his body, nor attached to the nectar the moon is pouring; neither disturbed by the impiety imparted by the lace of hacked heads round his neck, nor purified by the piety granted by the pious Gangajal; neither agitated by the ash besmearing his body nor titillated by the touch of Gauri's breasts. Lost in himself, ever joyous and healthy, such a Lord is He.

Lord Shankar's one epithet is Shiv, which means auspicious or all that is good. It means the Lord is the Destroyer of all that is wicked and Preserver of all that is fair and good. Thus, in a way he is responsible for not only destruction of the wicked creation but also for the preservation of noble creation. That is, he assumes the role of Vishnu and, as asserted by Goswami Tulsidas, there is no difference between Vishnu and Lord Shankar. It appears as if, these divinities, signify the various functions of nature and change role according to the need of the circumstances.

The carnal details concerning this Great Lord are the following. His dwelling places are Kashi and Kailash Mount, his wife is Uma or Gauri (second wife); he has two sons named Ganesh and Kartikeya. Some of the Puranas say that he was also the father of Lord Hanuman. He loves to have narcotic drugs like Bhang (Cannabis Indica), Ganja, etc. The things offered at his linga during worship are ber (Indian berries), vilvapatra (Wood Apple Leaves), Aak (a poisonous plant having white milk like substance) and of course, milk.

Lord Shiv epitomises all that a human mind could imagine in choosing a god. That is why he appears to be a concept of contradictions. But one thing is clear. He doesn't want all paraphernalia that Lord Vishnu is supposed to care for. Lord Shiv is a complex yet a simple god who is alike for all: whether the worshipper is demon or man or ghost. He is really Mahadeva or the Grand deity.

II. Lord Shiv in the Mythological Legends

Lord Shiv has been variously described in scores of Puranas, Mahabharat and other books but the main source is 'Shiv Purana'. Some of the important happenings have been described below.

Sati-Prasang (Sati-Episode) :—Sati or Shakti was the first wife of Lord Shiv. She was the daughter of Daksha-Prajapati. Once when Lord Shiv and Shakti were returning from the hermitage of sage Agastya, who recounted them the Rama-Tale, they happened to find Rama and Lakshman roaming about the jungle and searching for Sita. Lord Shiva spotted both the brothers from a distance and bowed reverentially before Rama. Now Sati or Shakti, moving with Lord Shiv, was rather surprised to see her Espouse, a Great God in His own right, bowing in esteem before the son of a mortal king. She had no idea that Ram was an incarnation of Lord Vishnu and had come on to the earth to redeem it from the demon-menace. When they started moving again, she asked her husband as to why did he bow before the son of a mortal king. Smilingly Lord Shiv replied that Ram was an incarnation of Lord Vishnu. "Then why he is crying like a mortal being for his wife who has been abducted by Ravana, the demon king. Being God Himself he knows well the reality. Why is he pretending like a mortal being and making also his younger brother unhappy. Why this drama?" she asked rather disbelievingly. Lord Shankar tried to impress upon her explaining the cause of his showing utter respect to Ram but she was not convinced. Then the Lord said, "Well, if you doubt then why don't you test my lord (Ram) yourself". Sati was ready to do so. So leaving her Lord, she went ahead in the jungles, thinking how should she test Lord Ram. Then, brooding over, she hit upon a brilliant idea.

"Why should not I adopt Sita's form. I know how she looked like as I remember clearly whatever the sage had described about her. This way, I will be able to test this prince better. If he is really an incarnation of Lord Vishnu, he would see through my game and recognise me instantly. And in case he fails to do so, then I would know that he is an ordinary mortal being. Moreover, my testing this prince this way is for my advantage. If he is really the Great God as I was told by my husband, his Darshan would definitely ensure my welfare. If not, then I would have proved my point before my husband." Thinking so, she moved on adopting Sita-like semblance.

But Rama exposed her instantly. The moment she came before him, he sweetly asked: "O Devi? Why are you roaming about the jungles all alone? Where is your husband and my Lord Shankar?"

Satisfied, she returned. But Lord Shankar had known by his intuition about Shakti's adopting Sita's form. Now, Sati had become unacceptable to him as his wife owing to latter's putting up a form of someone who was mother-like to him. Shiv always regarded Sita as someone equivalent to his mother in status. And with this thought Shiv mentally severed all relationship with his wife, deeming her to be his mother.

All this while Sati was ignorant of Shiv's this decision. It was revealed to her only when Shiv, on Shakti's reaching near him, offered her a seat in front of him and not on his left side, as was customary. This was enough of an indication of Shiv's resolve to desert her wife privately though for the outward world they were still an inseparable pair. Sati was passing through a great mental agony. All the time she wept privately but outwardly tried to appear normal. Her main complaint was that how could she lose her total personality by adopting a guise of someone else for a short while. It was only a stage act. How could she lose her ownself by being someone for a few moments? These types of theatrical performance had been witnessed by her Espouse in the past many a time. When

11

Vishnu, the Grand Lord, adopted the guise Mohini to hood-wink the demons for the god's cause, but no body took him to be an enchantress permanently. All considered him not Mohini but the real Lord as he had always been. "Why, then, my doing Sita's role for a while made me lose my original self so much so that even my husband had deserted me, deeming me to be Sita! It is not fair, Lord!" But her private agony had no relief. Shiv was lost in meditation and the world was moving on its rut, uncaring for the tremendous torture she was undergoing.

Then one day, Shiv came out of his meditative trance, singing hymns. When she went near him, he greeted her with not an affectionate but reverent look. For she was now equivalent to his mother in status! Crestfallen she returned. Then she happened to glance upwards and saw a big group of the "Vimanas" going southwards. Upon enquiry from an assistant, she learnt that her father Daksha had arranged a huge sacrifice (Yagya) after becoming the Prajapati (Progenitor).

Now Sati was thrilled. She decided to go to attend the sacrifice although not invited. But when she asked her Lord, he replied: "I admit that one doesn't need an invitation to go to one's father's place, but going there uninvited on some special occasion is not proper. I am surprised that in his anger at me your father has even forgotten to invite you, his own daughter!" But Sati wasn't convinced and said that her father may nurse a grudge against them but when she had no animosity, there was no harm in her going to attend the sacrifice on her own. At last, Shiv allowed her to go to attend the Sacrifice.

But when she reached the venue she was aghast to observe the reaction of her sisters and father. They showed utter contempt for her. Only her mother met her with some affection. But Sati had more painful surprises for her in store. As she reached near the altar, she was enraged seeing that no offering was made for her Lord Shankar, the Chief Deity and a God of the Trinity. Despite her being disowned by her husband, it was too much for her to tolerate this public insult to her husband by her own father. She felt so angry and disturbed that she decided to sacrifice her life by immolating herself in the holy fire of the altar.[1] Her death created great disturbance there. The henchmen of Lord Shiv, who had come escorting her to the Sacrifice-venue, returned to Mount Kailash with the sad news. Lord Shiv blew up in rage. In his uncontrollable anger, Lord Shiv uprooted his one-matted hair and dashed it against the rock. And out emerged from it a deadly existence Veerbhadra who was despatched by Lord Shiv with a huge army to avenge his beloved spouse Sati's death. They created such a massive havoc there that the whole sacrifice was ruined with many holy seers and Daksha's face got disfigured. Even the help provided by Vishnu and other gods was of no avail. Atlast, by other gods' effort Daksha came and bowed before Lord Shiv and that disturbance was quelled.

Now Shiv felt great agony for his dead wife. No doubt he loved her immensely but had to give her up as wife as she tried to adopt Sita's form. But that didn't lessen her love for her. Her untimely death made Shiv almost mad in her love and taking Sati's dead body upon his shoulders he began to dance his weird Tandav Dance. His foot-step's voilent thrust imbalanced the whole realms. Not only earth but heaven and pataal were also received massive jolts. But who was to control a frenzic Shiv? At last, on the seers' and gods' priest Jupiter's advice, Vishnu hacked the body of Sati to pieces. Wherever these pieces fell, there stands now a Shaktipeetha. When the body was totally hacked off to pieces, Shiv's agony abetted a little. Then he went inside the cave and began to mediate, getting totally averse to the world and its attractions.

There, the demon's mother had produced a demon named Vajrang. He was very powerful and soon began to torture gods. At last they managed to slay him with Vishnu's help. But Vajrang's son Tarak was a deadly demon who had grown very

1. This act came to be known as becoming a Sati.

powerful. He was tormenting the gods ruthlessly. All the gods were running here and there in the dread of the demon but couldn't get protection. Ultimately they sought counsel from Brahma. It was Brahma who had granted the boon of invincibility to that demon. So he said: "I know my boon can be flouted by Lord Shankar's son. But after the death of his first wife he had grown averse to worldly matters. You must try to arouse Shiv's passion and make him agree to marry Himachalraj and Maina's daughter Parvati, who is no one else but Shakti in this life. Uma or Parvati is the incarnation of Shakti. She has taken a vow that she would marry only Shiv. In fact, she is destined to marry someone who is a homeless, undressed ascetic-type of a person. Narad said "only Shiv is like that, in whom all these negative attributes have grown in a most positive manner. Parvati is doing rigorous penance to get Shiv as her husband. But Shiv has now grown totally averse to passion. You all must plan in such a way as to arouse his passion, possibly by making Kam to cast his spell."

As advised by Brahma, all the gods despatched Kam, the god of love, to cast his spell on Shiv. Lord Shiv was sitting in meditation. Lord of Love, Kamdeva, reached there with his accoutrements which included the bow and arrow made of flowers. Aiming one of the arrows, after having charged it with his hynotic spell, he threw it at Lord Shiv's head where it struck softly but enough to disturb meditation of Lord Shiv. The Lord felt angry so much so that a fiery eye appeared in the middle of his forehead. And out emerged from it a beam of scorching heat which incinerated the body of Kam there and then. This made the gods greatly grieved. Now, their whole plan had been upset. So far, Kam had been their most effective weapon. But now he had been incinerated. What should they do, they began to brood. Then Rati, the wife of Kam reached there, crying bitterly. The gods, led by her, reached before Shiv. Rati wept so bitterly before the kind-hearted Lord Shiv that the Lord said: "Although your husband has lost his body, yet he will exist bodylessly. He would regain his body in the Dwapar Age when he will be born as a son to Shree Krishna and Rukmini, and his name will be Pradyumna." Saying so, Lord Shiv, after many requests from the gods agreed to marry Parvati, who had been firmly observing severe penance to get Lord Shankar as her husband despite many a test to hoodwink her by gods and sages conducted on Lord Shiv's suggestion. At last she had her wish fulfilled and she got married to Lord Shiv with great pomp and fanfare onthe fourteenth day of the bright fortnight of the month Margsheersha. That day is still celebrated as the Shivratri festival. After marriage Parvati begot Kartikeya, who had six faces. When still a child he was made the commander-in-chief of the divine forces and ultimately he slayed the demon Tarak.

Parvati and Shiv also begot another son Ganesh. This son was born when Shiv was out in a cave, meditating. Once the goddess Parvati had gone to take bath with her friends Jaya-Vijay and made her child stand guarding the gate. When Lord Shiv came, the boy refused to allow him to go in. Since Lord Shiv was unaware who that boy was, he was enraged. Then a battle ensued in which Lord Shiva happened to hack off the head of his this son. When Parvati heard the commotion she came out and seeing her son beheaded summoned her deadly forces to slay all the gods. At last, with Lord Vishnu's intervention, she becalmed only after getting the boon from Lord Shiv that her beheaded son be again made to live. She also took the boon that among all the gods her son should always be worshipped first. Lord Shiv then transplanted the head of a one tusked elephant on his beheaded son and called him Ganesh, the lord of Ganas or Shiv's henchmen. Since then all worships start with the worship of Ganesh.

(There are innumerable stories of mythological origin woven round Lord Shiv and his family. The interested reader should consult 'Shiv-Puran' (Diamond Publication) for getting the full stories. The gist has already been given above).

III. The Twelve Seats of Lord Shiv (or the Jyotirlingas)

It is mentioned in the Shiv-Purana that Lord Shiva has twelve important places all over Bharatavarsha where He dwells in his linga form. Although there are uncountable Shiv Mandirs not only in India but abroad also, these twelve places have special significance for the devotees of Lord Shiv. These places and how they came to be recognised as the Seat of Shiv have been described below:-

1. **Shree Somnath:**— Situated on the western sea-coast in Gujarat, this place is a hollowed seat for the Shiv-worshippers. This has reference in the Mahabharat, Skanda Purana and Shiv-Purana. According to the mythological legend, Daksha Prajapati had 27 daughters and all were married to Chandrama, the moongod. Rohini was the most beautiful dame among these 27 and Chandrama was specially attached to her. This made her other sisters very jealous and they complained about Chandrama's partially to their father Daksha. But when he tried to impress upon Chandrama, the former didn't heed to his counsel. Enraged, Daksha cursed Chandrama that he be afflicted with Rajyakshama (T.B.). And soon Chandrama began to lose his shine and power. The gods were unhappy to see the nights getting darker and darker. They requested Daksha to reduce the intensity of the curse. Then Daksha said, "All right. If he promises to perform the puja of Mahadev ji at the Prabhas Kshetra, he may get back his shine for the remaining half of the month." Chandrama did so. Since then the moon started to wax and wane alternately. Since he (his one of the name in Som also) performed the puja, that site began to be called Somnath and Lord Shiv acquired one more epithet. On every

16

Shravan Poornima (full moon-night between mid-July to mid-August) a great festival is held there. The main station is Verawal from where Somnath is just 6 kms. away.

2. **Kedarnath:**—This holy shrine amidst high Himalayas is a very sacred place. It is near Badrinath and devotees visit both the places. It is said that Badrinath pilgrimage brings no merit if one doesn't go to Kedarnath. It is because of a legend; which is described below.

Long-long ago, there were two great seers called Nar and Narayan. They had performed a severe penance ot propitiate Mahadev ji who eventually blessed the seers. These two seers have their shrines at Badrinath. Since Kedarnath is the place where Lord Shiv appeared to bless Nar-Narayan whose shrines are at Badrinath, it is obvious that Lord Badrinath (Nar and Narayan) would not be propitiated unless their chosen deity is also revered. For going to Kedarnath one has to go to Rishikesh in U.P. From there one can get regular buses, etc., to reach Kedarnath. Kedarnath has no idol or linga. A huge triangular boulder is jutting out which is adored and worshipped by the devout by smearing ghee (clarified butter) on it.

3. **Shri Vishwanath**:—Varanasi is not only an ancient city of India but perhaps one of the oldest cities of the world, and has been one of the greatest religious-cultural centre of the east. It is mentioned in the Puranas hat even during the Final Dissolution (Pralaya) this city doesn't vanish, and Lord Shiv holds it safe on the point ofhis trident. It is said that Varanasi was the fist land-spot where the Creation began or begins after the Dissolution. It was here that Lord Vishnu performed great penance to begin the Creation a new and had propitiated Lord Shankar with this intention. Lord Shankar appeared there at Lord Vishnu's request. That spot, now amidst the maze of tiny lanes and by-lanes, has the Vishwanath Temple with many Dharamshalas/hotels, etc., for pilgrims stay. Varanasi is well connected by air, rail and bus route with all the major cities of the country.

4. **Sri Mahakaleshwar:**—The ancient city of Ujjaiyani,now Ujjain, is one of those seven holy cities, journey to which ensures Moksha, so delcare the Puranas. This temple of Mahakal is situated here. According to Shiv Purana, the story of its existence is as follows.

There lived a very pious and religious man in a town of Avantika. He had four sons. When the town was terrorised by a demon called Bhoosan, the brahman sacrificed the life of his one of the sons. At his great scrifice Lord Shiv appeared there Since then the temple came into existence.

There is also a legend attached to the origin of this place It is said that in ancient times the zero degree longitude time for time zone used to pass through Ujjaiyani. Since Shiv is the Lord who rules over time, the shrine came to be known as Mahakala-Temple or the Temple of TIME.

Ujjaiyani is well connected with Indore and Delhi by rail route, and is now an important city of Madhya Pradesh.

5. **Shree Omkareshwar:**—It is also situated in Madhya Pradesh on the Ratlam-Khandwa section of the railways. There is a small station named Omkareshwar Road which is not far off from the shrine. Near this shrine the river Kaveri joins Narmada. For reaching the shrine the devotees have to cross the river Narmada by boat. Passing between two hills, Narmada looks enchanting in its majestic beauty. The colour of the boulder and rock is bright copper which lend more charm to the spectacle.

The temple is situated on the hill or mount called Mandhata. Mandhata was the famous Suryavanshi king who had performed great penance here to propitiate Lord Shankar.Pleased by the devout king's worship, Lord Shankar appeared before him to grant his desired boon. Then the king had a temple built around the site where Lord had appeared Here, in the sanctum sanctorum of the temple, there is a natural black stone appearing like a tortoise, which is the symbol of Lord Shiv. Here the devout offer bilva-patra and flower gar lands, including the leaves of Tulsi. It is said that whatever water or milk, etc., that is poured on the symbol goes down straight to the river Narmada. Nearby this temple is also a famous shrine dedicated to Lord Shiv, called Amleshwar. It is held that the two shrines are complementary to each other and worshipping at both the shrines brings to the devotee the full merit by the grace of Lord Shankar.

6. **Shree Mallikarjun:**—It is situated in Tamilnadu, on the bank of Krishna river; on the mount Shail, which is also called the 'Kailash of South'. Mahabharat says that worshipping Lord Shankar at the Shail Mount grants the devotee the merit which might accure to one after performing the Ashwamedha Yagya. This place is also a famous Shaktipeetha (the Principal Seat of Shakti, the Goddess). It is said that here, in the mythological times, Lord Ganesh and Kartikeya developed a dispute as who should be worshipped first. Lord Shankar then declared that he who make seven round of the world fastest shall deserve the honour. But Lord Ganesh won as he moved seven times round his parents saying that parents meant whole world to him. This shrine is situated amidst dense jungle and accessible mostly during the 'Shivratri' festival, that too for a large group. For no one should go here alone. For coming here one should come upto Kurnool station on Manmad-Kachiguda line, from where buses are available on the festival occasion.

7. **Shree Baijnath Dham:**—This famous shrine is near Jasideeha in Bihar which is on Howrah-Patna lines. It is said that once Ravan prayed Lord Shankar to go to Lanka. Lord said that he would, provided he carried his linga non-stop to Lanka. Since the gods were not willing that Lord Shiv should to go to Lanka, they made water-god Varuna to enter Ravan's stomach and urge him to urinate. Unable to control his bladder, Ravan was forced to keep the linga on the ground. Then he couldn't lift it, as Lord had asked him to carry it non-stop to Lanka. This linga is specially important for bringing water from all the holy places and pouring it over it. The 'Kanwar'

carrying people throng this place on the Shravan Poornima (August end) day.

8. **Shree Bhimshankar:**—Situated on the mount of the range Sahayadri, this is quite inaccessible a place, which can be reached only around Shivratri festival by bus from Poona. After slaying Tripurasur demon Lord Shankar had taken rest here. Here, an old ruler of the Avadh region, named Bhimak was performing great worship to propitiate Lord Shankar. When the Lord reached here, he granted the desired boon to Bhimak and said that this shrine would be famous by his name. For coming here one can go take a bus to some distance then the remaining portion of the distance (63 kms.) has to be covered on foot.

9. **Dhushmeshwar:**—On the Central Railway Section, on Manmad-Poorna line, there is a big station Daulatabad. From Daulatabad, 12 miles away, there is a small village Vaisal. One can get conveyance from Daulatabad to reach the shrine. It is said that there were two sisters Sudeha and Dhushma, married to the same man. Dhushma was an ardent devotee of Lord Shankar and she used to make Lord Shankar's idol (linga) and after worship she had it dissolved in a pond. When she had completed 101 lingas Lord Shiv appeared there. Since then the shrine is called Dhushmeshwar Mahadeva.

10. **Triyambkeshwar**:—Situated in Nasik district of Maharashtra, it is on the main Delhi-Bombay line, just 12 kms. from Panchavati, the place Ravan had abducted Sita from. The origin of Godavari, the mount Brahmagiri, is not far off.

Here, when Jupiter transits in Leo sign, a huge Kumbha fair is held. Here, the Lord, is said to have appeared when the sage Gautam performed rigorous worship. Here are three lingas which represent the three Deities of Trinity. The scriptures forbid ladies coming here for 'Darshan'.

11. **Nageshwar:**—It is accessible from Dwarika (the famous holy city in Gujarat associated with Lord Krishna) by bus. The legend says that Lord Shankar appeared here when his

ardent devotee Supriya was about to be killed by a demon. Since Supriya had genuine faith, the Lord appeared there in answer to his prayer and slayed the demon. This is a small temple but on Shivratri day thousands of devotees come here.

12. **Setubandha Rameshwar:**—This famous shrine is the place where Lord Rama had worshipped Lord Shankar before slaying Ravana. It was only after Lord Shiv had granted Ramchandra the boon of victory that he could slay Ravana who was an ardent devotee of Lord Shankar. The linga is believed to have been made of the sea-sand. The shrine has 24 holy wells, where the devout take bath before the 'Darshan' of the Lord's linga.

IV. Rudraksha: The Eye of Lord Shiv

Rudraksha is a little bead grown on the tree called 'Utra Swam Bead Tree'. It is specially associated with Lord Shiv and due to its this association it has also acquired a mystical hallow round it. Literally it means the eye of Shiv. The 'Shiv-Puran' says that once Lord Shiv sat in meditation for a thousand years but failed to achieve his desired concentration. In a sense of desperation he closed his eyes with some force. And out emerged from his eyes a few drops of water or tears which fell on the ground. It is said that after falling to the ground they got germinated and resulted in the growth of a tree whose seed is what is known as Rudraksha. This priced bead is a mystified object with many curative qualities. It is also used as a charm or talisman to get one's desires fulfilled.

Botanically speaking, this tree is of medium height and generally found in the valley areas of Himalayas. Its leaves are small and round in shape. The seed of this tree: "Utra Swam Bead Tree" is the fabled rudraksha, known in different regions and languages by different names. In Hindi and Sanskrit it is called Aksha, Rudraksha, Shivaaksha, Neelkantaksha, Hari Haraksha and in Bengali Rudrakya; In Marathi and Gujarati Rudraksha and in Tamil 'Akkam'. In English it is Utra Swam Bead.

The masters of Ayurveda say that this in taste is sour, destroyer of wind in the stomach, a cure for the diseases connected with phlegmatic disorders and a good appetiser. In curing diseases connected with head it is specially very effective. The seed is to be rubbed on a honey-wet surface and the paste is to be consumed to make it show its curative effects. For all sorts of skin diseases, application of this paste is also very effective. Besides this, a lace made up of the beads, if worn as a necklace, also works wonders in the case of skin diseases. The wearer of this bead remains immune to many skin and mental diseases.

For blood pressure disorders rudraksha acts as a sure remedy. The wearer of the rudraksha or its lace gets his blood pressure soon normalised. Those with high B.P. should not only wear a rudraksha lace but also drink the water these beads have been soaked overnight in. If one regularly drinks this water, all problems connected with the blood-pressure get cured. The heart patient should wear the lace around neck. It is quite possible that owing to Rudraksha's these curative qualities this has been accorded such devotional status. The worshippers of Lord Shiv deem these beads as divine. They are extremely dear to Lord Shiv and his no worship is deemed complete unless Rudraksha is used in the ritual or worshipped separately. It is said:

बिना भस्य त्रिपुण्डेन, बिना रुद्राक्ष मालया।
पूजितोऽपि महादेवो, न स्यात् तस्य फलप्रद:।।

This bead has amazing qualities. The wearer of the bead-lace cannot be disturbed by any kind of evil spirits, nor any black magic could affect such a person. This bead or its lace should be worn after ritually bathing oneself and doing Lord Shiv's worship. Then while pronouncing the Panchaakshar Mantra (Om Namah Shivayaya) this bead-lace should be worn either on the wrist or round the neck. For making its lace the thread should be either a thin gold or silver chain or the cotton red or yellow thread. Wearing it in the gold or silver ring is also recommended.

Normally, in the India sub-continent four-coloured rudraksha: white, red, yellow and black, are available According to the old school, yellow is for the brahmans, red for the kshatriyas, white for the vaishya and black for the shudras are recommended. But there is no such hard or fast rule. Anyone can wear any type but only consideration should be that it shouldn't be broken, disfigured, moth-eaten or artificial. That bead which is firm, smooth and thick is considered best. A simple test of good rudraksha bead is to test it on the touchstone. Like rubbing of gold leaves a line on it, so a good rudraksha should also do.

The quality of the bead of rudraksha is also determined by the holes it has. These holes are called the 'Mukh' or mouth of the lead. Although there can be rudraksha having even 21 holes, normally available are of 14 holes. They have been described below.

1. **Ekamukhi Rudraksha** (One-hole Rudraksha): In the Tantrik-studies, this is considered to be the ultimate. The Tantrik who owns it has everything he wants. He who has it gets everything he desires: riches, comforts, recognition and honour. One simple test of the genuineness of such bead is this: if you put it in a cup filled with water, after half an hour or so, you will find the temperature of water raised. The wearer of this rudraksha is always cheerful, happy and contented. For chronic asthamatic patients wearing of this rudraksha works wonders. This is a very special bead and one who has it has everything-so say the old treatise of Ayurveda.

2. **Dwimukhi Rudraksha** (Two-hole Rudraksha): According-ing to the old treatise on the subject, this bead is a symbol of 'Ardhanareeshwa'. For the devotees of Shiv cult, this is a 'must' as it ensures the favour of Goddess Parvati also. Those who are troubled more by vile thoughts, obscene imagination and uncontrolled sexual lust should wear it.

3. **Trimukhi Rudraksha** (Three-hole Rudraksha): This is deemed to be fiery in temperament. Those who are troubled by phlegmatic disturbance should wear it. Its paste obtained by rubbing it on a surface wettened by milk is especially good to get rid of eye-troubles like trachoma, etc.

4. **Chaturmukhi Rudraksha** (Four-hole Rudraksha): This

is believed to symbolise Brahma, the Creator. It is recommended especially for those having proceative problems or memory loss. Boiling it in milk and drinking the decocted solution sharpens one's memory.

5. **Panchamukhi Rudraksha** (Five-hole Rudraksha): This represents Lord Shiv Himself. It is easily available in the market. The wearer of it is supposed to become immune to toxic effect caused either by insect bite or by wrong diet.

6. **Shadmukhi Rudraksha** (Six-hole Rudraksha): This is supposed to symbolise Lord Ganapati or Ganesh. For getting cure of the mental ailments, female deseases and enhancing ones's business acumen this bead is very effective.

7. **Saptamukhi Rudraksha** (Seven-hole Rudraksha): This represents Seven Matrishaktis. As a protective talisman this is ideal. If one finds one falling on evil days or astrologically speaking, one's bad pahse or Sade Saati is about to begin, wearing of this Rudraksha will provide the required protection.

8. **Asthamukhi Rudraksha** (Eight-hole Rudraksha): This represents the Eight-Armed Goddess or Asthabhuja Devi. In speculation this is supposed to render great help.

9. **Navamukhi Rudraksha** (Nine-hole Rudraksha): This also represents Devi Bhagwati and supposed to ensure success in litigation, etc. The heart-patients should also wear it.

10. **Dashmukhi Rudraksha** (Ten-hole Rudraksha): This bead is supposed to be the symbol of Yam, the death-god, and is now very rare. The Tantriks adore it as he who possesses it cannot have any adverse effect of other's black manoeuvres, and is always safe from accidents.

11. **Ekadashmukhi Rudraksh** (Eleven-hole Rudraksha): This rare bead is ideal for women. It is supposed to ensure happy marriedhood and very promising male issues.

12. **Dwadashmukhi Rudraksha** (Twelve-hole Rudraksha): Again a rare bead, this is ideal for the hermits and those who maintain the vow of continence.

13. **Trayodashmukhi Rudraksha** (Thirteen-hole

Rudraksha): This bead, now very rare, is believed to enhance one's sexual power tremendously as it is said to represent Kamdev. A favourite of Mughal Emperors, this is also supposed to be a very effective cure for venereal diseases.

14. **Chaturdashmukhi Rudraksha** (Fourteen-hole Rudraksha): Again a rare bead, this represents Lord Hanuman. The wearer is supposed to become very powerful and go beyond the effect of any mortal trouble. For he or she always have Lord Hanuman warding off the likely troubles.

27

V. शिव-स्तुतियाँ, स्तोत्र इत्यादि

नागेन्द्रहाराय त्रिलोचनाय
    भस्माङ्गरागाय महेश्वराय।
नित्याय शुद्धाय दिगम्बराय
    तस्मै 'न' काराय नमः शिवाय।। 1।।

जिनके कष्ठ में सापों का हार है, जिनके तीन नेत्र हैं, भस्म ही जिनका अङ्गराग (अनुलेपन) है; दिशाएं ही जिनका वस्त्र हैं (अर्थात् जो निरावरण हैं) उन शुद्ध अविनाशी महेश्वर 'न' काररूप शिव को नमस्कार है।। 1।।

मन्दाकिनी सलिल चन्दन चर्चिताय
    नन्दीश्वर प्रमथनाध महेश्वराय।
मन्दार पुष्प बहुपुष्प सुपूजिताय
    तस्मै 'म' काराय नमः शिवाय।। 2।।

मन्दाकिनी (गंगा) जल और चन्दन से जिनकी अर्चना हुई है, मन्दार-पुष्प तथा अन्यान्य कुसुमों से जिनकी सुन्दर पूजा हुई है, उन नन्दी के अधिपति प्रमयगणों के स्वामी महेश्वर 'म' काररूप शिव को नमस्कार है।। 2।।

शिवाय गौरी वदना ब्जवृन्द-
    सूर्याय दक्षाध्वरनाशकाय।
श्री नील कण्ठाय वृषध्वजाय
    तस्मै 'शि' काराय जयरु शिवाय।। 3।।

जो कल्याण स्वरूप हैं, पार्वती के मुखकमल को विकसित (प्रसन्न) करने

V. Hymns and Orisons in the Praise of Lord Shiv

Shree Shivpanchakshar Strotra
(The 'Five Letter's Hymn)

Nagendraharaya Trilochanaya
Bhasmangaragaya Maheshwaraya |
Nityaya Shuddhaya Digambaraya
Tasmai 'Na'[1] Karaya namah Shivalya | | 1 | |

He whose neck is gorlanded by snakes, who has three eyes, the ash only smears his body, wh is unclad, - 1 bow to Him, the pious, indestructible Lord Shiva in the form of 'Na'.

Mandakini salila chandan charchitaya
Nandishwar pramathnath maheshwaraya |
Mandar pushpa bahupushpasu supoojitaye
Tasmai 'Ma' karaye Namah Shivaya | | 2 | |

He who is annointed with the Ganga water and sandalwood paste; who has been worshipped with Mandar and other beautiful flowers; that Lord of Nandi and other henchmen, the Grand Lord Shiva-I bow to him in his 'Ma' form.

Shivaya Gauri vandana bjavrinda-
Sooryaya Dakshadhwarnashkaya |
Shru Neelkanthaya Vrishadhwajaya
Tasmai "Shi" karaya Namah Shivaya | | 3 | |

Who is of auspicious form; who acts like the rising sun to

---

1. All the five letters; Na, ma, shi, va, ja that appear in these five verses combinedly write 'Nama Shivaya'–meaning. I bow to Lord Shiva.

के लिए जो सूर्यरुप हैं, जो दक्ष का नाश करनेवाले हैं, जिनकी ध्वजा में बैल का चिन्ह है, उन शोभाशाली नीलकण्ठ 'शि'कार स्वरुप शिवजी को नमस्कार है।। 3।।

वशिष्ठ कुम्मोदभ्भ गौतमार्य-
    मुनीन्द्र देवार्चित शेखराय।
चन्द्रार्क वैश्वानर लोचनाय
    तस्मै 'व' काराय नमः शिवाय।। 4।।

वशिष्ठ, अगस्त्य और गौतम आदि श्रेष्ठ मुनियों ने तथा इन्द्रादि देवताओं ने जिनके मस्तक की पूजा की है; चन्द्रमा सूर्य और अग्नि जिनके नेत्र हैं, उन 'व' कारस्वरुप शिव को नमस्कार है।। 4।।

यक्षस्वरूपाय जटाधराय
    पिनाक हस्ताय सनातनाय।
दिव्याय देवाय दिगम्बराय
    तस्मै 'य' काराय नमः शिवाय।। 5।।

जिन्होंने यक्ष रुप धारण किया है, जो जटाधारी है, जिनके हाथ में पिनाक है, जो दिव्य सनातन पुरुज हैं, उन दिगम्बर देव 'य' कार स्वरूप शिव को नमस्कार है।। 5।।

पञ्चाक्षरमिंदपुण्यं यः पठेच्छिवसन्निधौ।
    शिव लोकवाप्नोति शिवेन सह मोदिते।

जो शिव के समीप इस पवित्र पञ्चाक्षर का पाठ करता है, वह शिव लोक को प्राप्त करता और वहाँ शिवजी के साथ आनन्दित होता है।

bloom the lotus-flower like face of Parvati ji, who is the destroyer of Daksha, whose flag has the bull-symbol, I bow to that blue throated Lord Shiva in his 'Shi' form.

Vashishtha kumbhodhava Gautamarya
Muneendra devarchita shekharaya |
Chandrarka Vaishwanar Lochanaya
Tasmai 'Va' karaya Namah Shivaya | | 4 | |

He who has been worshipped by the High sages like Vashishtha, Agastya and Gautam besides the other gods including Indra; whose eyes are the moon, the sun and the fire, I bow to that Lord Shiva in his 'va' form.

Yakshaswaroopaya Jatadharaya
Pinakhastaya sanatanaya |
Dwivyaya Devaya Digambaraya
Tasmai 'Ya' karaya Namah Shivaya | | 5 | |

He who has adopted the guise of Yaksha, who has long tendril hair, whose hand weilds a bow called Pinak, who is the Divine Eternal Man, I bow to unclad Deity Lord Shiva in his 'Ya' form.

Panchaksharmidam punyam yah pathechhivasannidhau |
Shivlokanavapnoti Shiven sah modite | | 6 | |

He who chants these verses glorifying five letters of the Incantation of the Lord, before the Lord, he attains the realm of Lord Shiva and lives ever blissfully with the Lord Shiva.

2. श्री शिव ताण्डव स्तोत्रम्

जटाटवी गलज्जल प्रवाह पावित स्थले
गलेऽवलम्ब्य लम्बितां भुजङ्ग तुङ्ग मालिकाम् ।
डम डुमड्डुमड्डुम न्निनादवड्डुमर्वयं
चकार चण्ड ताण्डवं तनोतु न: शिव: शिवम ।। 1 ।।

जिन्होंने जटारूपी अटवी (वन) से निकलती हुई गंगा जी के गिरते
हुए प्रवाहों से पवित्र किए गए गले में सर्पों की लटकती हुई विशाल माला
को धारण कर, डमरू के डम-डम शब्दों से मण्डित प्रचण्ड ताण्डव (नृत्य)
किया, वे शिव जी हमारे कल्याण का विस्तार करें ।। 1 ।।

जटाकटाह सम्भ्रम भ्रमन्नि लिम्प निर्झरी–
विलोल वीचि वल्लरी विराजमान मूर्ध्दनि ।
धगद्धगद्धग ज्ज्वलंल्ल लाट पट्टपावके
किशोर चन्द्रशेखरे रति: प्रतिक्षण मम ।। 2 ।।

जिनका मस्तक जटारूपी कड़ाह में वेग से घूमती हुई गंगा की चंचल
तरंग-लताओं से सुशोभित हो रहा है; लकाटाग्नि धक्-धक् जल रही है,
सिर पर बाल चन्द्रमा विराजमान है, उन (भगवान शिव) में मेरा निरंतर
अनुराग हो ।। 2 ।।

धराधरेन्द्र नन्दिनी विकास बन्धु बन्धुर–
स्फुरद्दिगन्त सन्तति प्रमोदमान मान से ।

2. Shree Shiv-Tandav Strotram
(Created by the Demon Lord Ravan)

Jatatavee galjjalapravah pavitasthale

Galeavalambya lamhitan bhujanga tunga malikam |

Damaddamaddamaddamaddamanninadavadda marvayam

Chakar Chand tandavam tanotu nah Shivah Shivam | | 1 | |

He who bore the gushing streams of the river Ganga through his matted locks' jungle, and thus purified, wore the galands of the snakes round his neck; who danced Tandava Dance on the beat of his celestial drum, the same Lord Shiv may ensure our welfare and enhance its ambit.

Jatakatah sambhram-bhramanni-limp nirjhari-

Vilol veechi vallari virajman moordhani |

Dhagaddhagadhagajjawallat pattapavake

Kishore Chandrashekhare ratih pratikshnan mum | | 2 | |

Whose forehead is resplendent amidst the fast moving streams of the river Ganga, appearing like the wave-ivys of the current in a cauldron of matted locks, whose light of the forehead is brightly lit, where head carries the nascent moon—to such Lord Shiva may my attachment be ever unwaning.

Dharadharendra nandini vilas bandhu bandhur-

Sphraddigant santati pramidman manse |

कृपा कटाक्ष घोरणी निरुद्धदुर्धरा पदि
क्वचि द्दिगम्बरे मनो विनोदमेतु वस्तुनि ।। 3 ।।

गिरिराज किशोरी पार्वती के विकास कालोपयोगी शिरोभूषण से समस्त दिशाओं को प्रकाशित होते देख जिनका मन आनंदित हो रहा है, जिनकी निरंतर कृपा दृष्टि से कठिन आपत्ति का भी निवारण हो जाता है, ऐसे किसी दिगम्बर तत्व में मेरा मन विनोद करे ।

जटाभुजंग पिंगल स्फुरत्फणामणिप्रभा
कदम्बकु ड्कुमद्रव प्रलिप्त दिग्व धूमुखे
मदान्धसिन्धु रस्फुरत्त्व गुत्तरीय मेदुरे
मनो विनोदमभ्दुतं बिभर्तु भूतभर्तरि ।। 4 ।।

जिनके जटाजूटवर्ती भुजंगमों (सर्पों) के फणों की मणियों का फैलता हुआ पिंगल (पीला) प्रभा पुंज दिशारूपिणी अङ्गनाओं (रमणियों) के मुख पर कुंकुमराग का अनुलेप कर रहा है, मतवाले हाथी के हिलते हुए चमड़े का उत्तरीय वस्त्र (चापट) धारण करने से स्निग्धवर्ण हुए उन भूतनाथ में मेरा चित्त अद्भुत विनोद करे ।

सहस्त्र लोचन प्रभृत्य शेष लेख शेखर–
प्रसूनधूलि धोरणी विधूसरा ड्घ्रि पठिभूः ।
भुजंग राज मालया निबद्धजाट जूटकः
श्रिये चिराय जायतां चकोरबन्धु शेखरः ।। 5 ।।

जिनकी चरण पादुका इन्द्र आदि समस्त देवताओं के (प्रणाम करते समय) मस्तकवर्ती कुसुमों की धूलि से धूसरित हो रही है; नागराज (शेष) के हार से बँधी हुई जटा वाले वे भगवान् चन्द्र शेखर मेरे लिए चिर स्थायिनी सम्पत्ति के साधक हों ।

Kripakatakchha dhorani Niruddhadurharapadi

Kwachiddigambare manovinodmetu vastuni | | 3 | |

Whose heart is delighted seeing the luxuriant head orna-
ments of the daughter of Mountain Parvati (his spouse) during
his love-play; whose constant favourable sight dispells even
the most severe catastrophe–he may engage my mind happily
in some such unfettered and uncovered delight.

Jatabhujanga pingalasphuratphanamani prabha-

Kadamba kumkumadrava pralipta digva dhoomukhe |

Madandhasindhurasphuratva guttariya mdure

Mano Vinodmadbhutam vibhartu bhootabhatari | | 4 | |

The yellowish glow emanating from the germs of the serpents dwelling in whose matted locks in making the visages
of the dames of the Quarter replendent with an enchanting
radiance; who is donning the skin of a 'must' elephant which
has made him look smooth complexioned–may in such Lord
of Beings my heart be ever engaged playfully.

Sahastra lochana prabhritya shesh lekha shekhar-

prasoondhooli dhorini vidhoosaran ghri peethabhuh |

Bhujang raj malaya Nibaddhajat jootakah:

Shriye Chiraya jayatam chakorbandhushekharah | | 5 | |

He, whose sandals are covered with the pollen of the flowers worn on their crowns by the gods including Indra at the
time of the celestials bowing to the Great Lord; he whose
tendril locks are bound by the coils of the Great Serpent 'Shesh'–
such Lord Chandrashekhar (Shiv, having moon on his head)
may ever enhance my prosperity and property.

ललाटचत्वर ज्वलद्धनञ्जय स्फुलिङ्गभा-
            निपति पञ्चसायकं नमन्निलम्पिनायकम् ।
सुधामयूख लेखया विराजमान शेखरं
            महाक पालि सम्पदे शिरो जटालमस्तु न: ।। 6 ।।

जिसने ललाट-वेदी पर प्रज्वलित हुई अग्नि के स्फुलिङ्गों के तेज से
कामदेव को नष्ट कर डाला था, जिसे इन्द्र नमस्कार किया करते हैं,
सुधाकर की कला से सुशोभित मुकुटवाला वह (श्री महादेव जी का) उन्नत
विशाल ललाटवाला जटिल मस्तक हमारी सम्पत्ति का साधक हो ।

कराल माल पट्टिका धगद्ध गद्धगज्ज्वल-
            द्धनञ्चयाहुतीकृत प्रचण्ड पञ्च सायके ।
धरा धरेन्द्र नन्दिनी कुचाग्र चित्र पत्रक-
            प्रकल्प नैक शिल्पि नि त्रिलोचने रतिर्मम ।। 7 ।।

जिन्होंने अपने विकराल भाजपट्ट पर धक्-धक् जलती हुई अग्नि में प्रचण्ड कामदेव
को हवन कर दिया था, गिरिराज किशोरी के स्तनों पर पत्र भङ्ग-रचना करने के
एकमात्र कारीगर उन भगवान त्रिलोचन में मेरी धारणा (ध्यान) लगी रहे ।

नवीन मेघमण्डली निरुद्धदुर्धर स्फर-
            त्कुहू निशीथिनी तम: प्रबन्धबद्ध कन्धर: ।
निलिम्प निर्झरीधरस्तनोतु कृति सिन्धुर:
            कलानिधान बन्धुर: श्रियं जगद्धुरन्धर: ।। 8 ।।

जिनके कण्ठ में नवीन मेघमाला से घिरी हुई अमावस्या की आधी रात
के समय फैलते हुए दुरूह अंधकार के समान श्यामता अंकित है। गजचर्म
लपेटे हुए हैं, वे संसारभाव को धारण करने वाले चन्द्रमा (के सम्पर्क) से
मनोहर कान्ति वाले भगवान गंगाधर मेरी सम्पत्ति का विस्तार करें।

Lalatachatvarajwaladdhananjayasphulinga bha-

Nipeeta panchasayakam namannilimpanayakam |

Sudhamayookha lekhaya virajman shekharam

Mahakapali sampade shiro jatalmastu nah || 6 ||

He whose forehead fire had incinerated Kamdeva (the lord of love); who is ever adored by Indra, who dons the moon as his diadem, may such Great Lord help us s enhancing our riches.

Karala bhalapáttika dhagaddhagaddhagajjwala-

Dhananjayahutikrita-prachanda panch sayake |

Dharadharendranadini kushagra chitra patraka-

Prakalpanaikashilpini trilochane ratirmum || 7 ||

He whose dazzling forehead strip had burned Kamdeva to ashes; who is the only artist to paint playfully on the beasts of the daughter of the Mountain–may my concentration be ever centred on such God with three eyes.

Naveen meghamandali niruddhadurdharsphur-

tkuhunisheethini tamah prabandhabaddha kan darah |

Nilimpa nirjhari dharastanotu krittasindhurah

Kalanidhan bandhurah shriyam jagatdhurandharah || 8 ||

Whose neck is bedight with the dark glaucuity witnessed by the gathering of rain-laden clouds at mid-night on the moon-less night; who is wrapped in the skin of an elephant, he, the preserver of the entire world, resplendent with the moon-shine, Lord, the Carrier of the Ganga, may ever enhance my riches.

37

प्रफुल्लनीलं पंकज प्रपञ्च कालि मप्रभा-

    वलम्बि कण्ठ कन्दली रुचि प्रबद्ध कन्धरम् ।

स्मरच्छिदं पुरच्छिदं भवच्छिदं मखच्छिदं

    गजच्छिदान्धकच्छिदं तमन्त कच्छि दं भजे ।। 9 ।।

जिनका कण्ठदेश खिले हुए नील कमलसमूह की श्याम प्रभा का अनुकरण करने वाली हरिणी की-सी छवि वाले चिन्ह से सुशोभित है तथा जो कामदेव, त्रिपुर, भव (संसार), दक्ष-यज्ञ, हाथी, अन्ध कासुर और यमराज का भी उच्छेदन करने वाले हैं, उन्हें मैं भजता हूँ ।

अखर्व सर्वमङ्गला कला कदम्ब मञ्जरी-

    रस प्रवाह माधुरी वि जृम्भणाम धुव्र तम् ।

स्मरान्तकं पुरान्तकं भवान्तकं मखान्तकं

    गजान्त कान्धकान्तकं तमन्त कान्त कं भजे ।। 10 ।।

जो अभिमान रहित पार्वती की कलारुप कदम्ब मंजरी के मकरन्द स्रोत की बढ़ती हुई माधुरी के पाने करने वाले मधुप हैं तथा कामदेव, त्रिपुर, भव, दक्ष-यज्ञ, हाथी, अन्धकासुर और यमराज का भी अंत करने वाले हैं, उन्हें मैं भजता हूँ ।

जयत्वदभ्रविभ्रमभ्रमभ्रदुजङ्गमश्वस-

    द्विनिर्गमत्क्रमस्फुरत्कराल भालहव्य वाट् ।

धिमि द्धिमि द्धिमि मिद् ध्वन न्मृदङ्ग तुङ्ग मङ्गल-

    ध्वनि क्रम प्रवर्तित प्रचण्ड ताण्डव: शिव: ।। 11 ।।

जिनके मस्तक पर बड़े वेग के साथ घूमते हुए भुजङ्ग के फुफकारने से ललाट की भयंकर अग्नि क्रमश: धधकती हुई फैल रही है; धिमि-धिमि बजते हुए मृदङ्ग के गम्भीर मङ्गल घोष के क्रमानुसार जिनका ताण्डव प्रचण्ड हो रहा है, उन भगवान शंकर की जय हो ।

Praphullaneela pankaja prapanch kalimaprabha-

Valambikanthakandali ruchi prabaddha kandharam |

Smarchhidam purachhidam bhava chhidam makhachhidam

Gaja chhidandhakachidam tamant kachhidam bhaje | | 9 | |

He whose neck-portion is bedight with a symbol like that of a doe following the glaucous glow of the bunch of the blue lotuses; he who is the destroyer of Kamdeva, Tripur, this world, the sacrifice arranged by Daksha, the elephant (to plant is head on his son Ganesh head), the Demon Andhakasur and even the god of death Yam—I chant his name only.

Akharvasarvamangla kala kadambamanjari

Rasapravah madhuri vijrimbhanam dhuvratam |

Smrantakam Purantakam bhavantakam Makhantakam

Gajanta kandha kantakam tamanta kantakam bhaje | | 10 | |

He who is the bee to enjoy the sap of the ever increasing dalliance of the flower of unconceited Parvati's amorous plays; who brings end of Kamdeva, Tripura, the world, the sacrifice arranged by Daksha, the elephant, the demon Andhakasur and even of Yamraj I chant his name only.

Jayatvadabhravibhrambhrambhadubjang mashvasha-

Dwinirgamatkramasphuratkaral bhal havyavat |

Dhimi ddhimi ddhimi dhwann mridang tunga mangala

Dhwani kram pravartita prachanda Tandavah Shivah | | 11 | |

The fast movement of the violently hissing serpents over his head is stoking the forehead fire dreadfully, and the profoundly auspicious sound of the drums is making his Tandava dance gain in faster beats. May such God Shankar be ever victorious!

दृष्टिद्विचित्र तल्प यो भुजङ्ग मौक्ति कस्रजो
गरिष्ठ रत्न लोष्ठयो: सुहृद्धि पक्ष पक्षयो: ।
तृणार विन्द चक्षुषो: प्रजा मही महेन्द्र यो:
सम प्रवृत्तिक: कदा सदा शिवं भजाम्यहम् ।। 12 ।।

पत्थर और सुन्दर बिछौनों में; साँप और मुक्ता की माला में; बहुमूल्य रत्न
तथा मिट्टी के ढेले में, मित्र या शत्रुपक्ष में; तृण अथवा कमल लोचना तरुणी में,
प्रजा और पृथ्वी के महाराज में समान भाव रखता हुआ मैं कब सदाशिव को भजूँगा?

कदा निलम्प निर्झरी निकुञ्जकोटरे वसन्
विमुक्त दुर्मति: सदा शिर: स्थमञ्जलिं वहन ।
विलोल लोल लोचनो ललामभाल लग्न क:
शिवेति मन्त्रमुच्चरन् कदा सुखी भवाभ्यहम ।। 13 ।।

सुन्दर ललाट वाले भगवान् चन्द्रशेखर में दत्तचित्त हो अपने कुविचारों को त्याग
कर गंगा जी के तटवर्ती निकुंज के भीतर रहता हुआ सिर पर हाथ जोड़ डबडबायी
हुई विक्लल आँखों से 'शिव' मन्त्र का उच्चारण करता हुआ मैं कब सुखी होऊँगा?

इमं हि नित्य मेव मुक्त मुत्त मोत्तमं स्तवं
पठन्स्मरन्ब्रुवन्नरो विशुद्धमेति सन्ततम ।
हरे गुरौ सुभक्ति माशु याति नान्यथा गतिं
विमोहन हि देहिनां सुशङ्करस्य चिंतनम् ।। 14 ।।

जो मनुष्य इस प्रकार से उक्त इस उत्तमोत्तम स्तोत्र का नित्य पाठ,
स्मरण और वर्णन करता रहता है, वह सदा शुद्ध रहता है और शीघ्र
ही सुरगुरु श्री शंकर की अच्छी भक्ति प्राप्त कर लेता है, वह विरुद्ध गति
को प्राप्त नहीं होता, क्योंकि शिव जी का अच्छी प्रकार का चिन्तन प्राणि
वर्ग के मोह को नाश करने वाला है।

Drishadwichitra talpayor-bhujangmaukti kasrajo-
rgarishtha ratna loshthayoh Suhridwipakaha pakshyoh |
Trinar vindachachakshushoh Prajamahee mahendra yoh
Sama pravrittikah kada sada Shivam bhajamyaham || 12 ||

Maintaining my equanimity amidst the bed of stones and cosy mattresses; amidst the pearl necklace and the snakes; amidst the gems or the clod of earth, amidst the firends or foes, amidst the dry straw and the lotus-eyed young ladies, amidst the masses and the Lord of Earth, when shall I worship Lord Shiv?

Kada nilampa nirjhari nikunjakotare vasan
Vimuktadurmatih sada shirastha manjali vahan |
Vilola lolaochano lalambhalla lagnakah
Shiveti mantramuccharan kada sukhi bhavamyaham || 13 ||

Concentrating totally my mind on the Great-God Chandrashekhar with bright forehead, and shunning my vile thoughts, dwelling inside a grove on the bank of river Ganga, when shall I be happy chanting the 'Shiv' Incantation with tear filled eyes, while keeping my bound hands upon my forehead?

Imam hi nitya meva mukta mottamam stvam
Pathansmaranbru vannaro vishuddhameti santatam |
Hare gurau subhaktimashu yatinanyatha gatim
Vimohanam hi dehinam Sushankarasya chintanam || 14 ||

He who reads, chants and remembers this best of the hymns, remains ever pure and soon attains the pious devotion of Lord Shankar, the Chief of Gods. He never faces adversity because the mere rememberance of Lord Shankar destroys all the infatuation inherent in the beings.

पूजावसान समये दशवक्त्रगीतं
य: शम्भु पूजन पर पठति प्रदोषे ।
तस्य स्थिरां रथ गजेन्द्र तुङ्गयुक्तां
लक्ष्मीं सदैव सुमुखीं प्रददाति शम्भु: ।। 15 ।।

सायं काल में पूजा समाप्त होने पर रावण द्वारा गाए हुए इस शम्भू पूजन सम्बन्धी स्तोत्र का जो पाठ करता है, भगवान शंकर उस मनुष्य को रथ, हाथी, घोड़ों से युक्त सदा स्थिर रहने वाली अनुकूल सम्पत्ति देते हैं ।

42

Poojavasan samaye dashvaktrageetam

Yah Shambhu poojan param pathati pradoshe |

Tasya sthiran rath gajendra tungamukta

Lakshmim sadaiva sumukheem prad-dati Shambhuh || 15 ||

At the conclusion of his evening worship, he who chants this hymn dedicated to Lord Shambhu and created by Ravana, receives chariots, elephants, horses and other riches whichever remian favourable to the persons by the grace of Lord Shankar.

3. श्री रुद्राष्टकम्

नमामीशमीशान   निर्वाणरूपं
विभुं व्यापकं ब्रहम वेदस्वरुपं ।
निजं निर्गुण निर्विकल्पं निरीहं
चिदाकाशमाकाशवासं भजे हं ।। 1 ।।

हे ईशान! मैं । मुक्तिस्वरूप, समर्थ, सर्वव्यापक, ब्रहम, वेदस्वरूप, निज
स्वरूप में स्थित, निर्गुण, निर्विकल्प, निरीह (इच्छा रहित) अनन्त ज्ञानमय
और आकाश के समान सर्वत्र व्याप्त प्रभु को प्रणाम करता हूँ ।

निराकार मोङ्कारमूलं तुरीयं
गिरा ग्यान गोतीतमीशं गिरीशं ।
करालं महाकाल कालं कृपालं
गुणा गार संसार पारं न तो हं ।। 2 ।।

जो निरंकार हैं, ओङ्कारूप आदिकारण हैं, तुरीय हैं, वाणी, बुद्धि
और इन्द्रिओं के पथ से परे हैं, कैलाश नाथ हैं, पापियों के लिए कराल
और भक्तों हेतु दयालु हैं, महाकाल के भी काल हैं; गुणों के आगार और
संसार से तारने वाले हैं, उन भगवान को मैं नमस्कार करता हूँ ।

3. Eight Verses in the Praise of Rudra (Shankar)
(Tulsidas-created)

Namamishamishan nirwanroopam

Vibhum vyapakam Brahm vedaswaroopam

Nijam nirgunam nirvikalpam nireeham

Chidakashmakashvasam bhaje ham

O Eeshan[1]! I bow to the Great Lord who is ever free, omniscient, all-pervading, Brahm, the manifestation of the Vedas, steady, ever-engrossed in the self-form, attributeless, all alone and desireless and with whom this whole universe is instinct.

Nirakaramonkar moolam tureeyam

Gira gyan goteetameesham gireesham

Karalam mahakal kalam kripalam

Gunagar sansar param natsaham

Who is formless, manifestation of Om, and the ultimate cause of this world; who is imperceptible by senses voice or wisdom, who is the Lord of Kailash; who is dreadful to the sinners and kind to his devotees; who is the Death of Time; the mine of all virtues and capable of taking one across this world– I bow to such Lord!

---

1. Literally north-east direction, believed to be the abode of Lord Shiva.

तुषाराद्रि संकाश गौरं गभीर
  मनोभूत कोटि प्रभा श्री शरीरं।
स्फुरन्मौलि कल्लोलिनी चारु गंगा
  लसद्भाल बालेन्दु कंठे भुजंगा।। 3 ।।

जो हिमालय के समान श्वेतवर्ण, गम्भीर और करोड़ों कामदेवों जैसे कान्तियान शरीर वाले हैं, जिनके मस्तक पर मनोहर गंगा लहरा रही है, मस्तक (भाल) पर बाल चन्द्रमा सुशोभित है और गले में सर्पों की माला शोभायमान है।

चलत्कुंडलं भ्रू सुनेत्रं विशालं
  प्रसन्नाननं नील कंठे दयालं।
मृगाधीश चर्माम्बरं मुण्डमालं
  प्रियं शंकरं सर्वनाथं भजामि।। 4 ।।

जिनके कानों में कुण्डल हिल रहे हैं, जिनके नेत्र एवम् भृकुटी सुन्दर और विशाल हैं, जिनका मुख प्रसन्न और कण्ठ नील है, जो बड़े ही दयालु हैं, जो बाघ ही खाल का वस्त्र और मुण्डों की माला पहनते हैं, उन सर्वनाथ (सबके स्वामी) प्रिय शंकर का मैं भजन करता हूँ।

प्रचंडं प्रकृष्टं प्रगल्भं परेशं
  अखण्डं अजं भानुकोटिप्रकाशं।
त्रयः शूल निर्मूलनं शूल पाणिं
  भजे हं भवानी पतिं भाव गम्यं।। 5 ।।

जो प्रचण्ड, सर्वश्रेष्ठ, प्रगल्भ, परमेश्वर पूर्ण, अजन्मा, कोटि सूर्य के समान प्रकाशमान, त्रिभुवन के शूल (कष्ट) नाशक और हाथ में त्रिशूल धारण करने वाले हैं, उन भावगम्य भवानी पति का मैं भजन करता हूँ।

Tusharadri sankash gauram gabheeram

Manobhooti koti prabha shree shareeram |

Sphurnmauli kallolini charu ganga

Lasatbhal balendu kanthe bhujanga | | 3 | |

He who is bright-complexioned like the Himalayas, pro-
found and his body-beauty is capable of outcharming millions
of the Kamdevas; upon whose head flowing pious Ganga river
and whose forehead is bedight with the nascent moon; whose
neck is encircled by the garlands of serpents.

Chalatkundalam bhroo sunetram vishalam

Prasannananam neelkantha dayalam |

Mrigadheesha charmambaram mundamalam

Priyam Shankaram savanatham bhajami | | 4 | |

Whose earrings are amove; whose eyes and eye brows are
big and beautiful; whose visage is cheerful and neck blue; who
is supremely kind, who dons panther-skin for clothes and a
necklace of hacked heads for ornament - I bow to such Lord,
Master of All, Supremely adorable Lord Shaṇkar, and chant his
name.

Prachandam prakrishtam pragalbham paresham

Akhandam ajam bhanukotiprakasham |

Trayah shool nirmoolanam shool pani

Bhajeaham bhavani patim bhav gamyam | | 5 | |

He who is Terrible, the Best, Omniscient, God, Complete,
Unborn, resplendent like millions of suns; the Destroyer of all the
afflictions of the Three realms, weilding a Trident in his hand—I
chant his name, the Lord of Bhavani, manifest by feeling.

कलातीत कल्याण कल्पान्तकारी
सदा सज्जना नन्ददाता पुरारी।
चिन्दानन्द संदोह मोहापहारी
प्रसीद प्रसीद प्रभो मन्मथारी।। 6।।

हे प्रभो! आप कला रहित, कल्याणकारी और कल्प का अन्त करने
वाले हैं। आप सर्वदा सत्पुरुषों को आनन्द देते हैं; आपने त्रिपुरासुर का
नाश किया था। आप मोहनाशक और ज्ञानानन्द घन परमेश्वर हैं। काम
देव आपके शत्रु हैं, आप मुझ पर प्रसन्न हों, प्रसन्न हों!

न यावद् उमानाथ पादार विन्दं
भजंतीह लोके परे वा नराणां।
न तावत्सुखं शान्ति संतापनाशं
प्रसीद प्रभो सर्व भूताधिवासं।। 7।।

मनुष्य जब तक उमापति महादेव जी के चरणाविन्दों का भजन नहीं
करते, उन्हें इहलोग या परलोक में कभी सुख और शान्ति की प्राप्ति नहीं
होती और न उनका संताप ही दूर होता है। हे समस्त भूतों के निवास
स्थान भगवान शिव आप मुझ पर प्रसन्न हों।

न जानामि योगं जपं नैव पूजां
नतोऽहं सदा सर्वदा शंभु तुभ्यं।
जरा जन्म दुःखौध तातप्यमानं
प्रभो पाहि आपन्नमामीश शंभो।। 8।।

हे प्रभो! हे शम्भो! हे ईश! मैं योग, जप और पूजा कुछ भी नहीं जानता!
हे शम्भो! मैं सदा-सर्वदा आपको नमस्कार करता हूँ। जरा, जन्म और
दुःखसमूह से सन्तप्त होते हुए मुझ दुःखी की दुःख से आप रक्षा कीजिए।

Kalateeta kalyan kalpantkari

Sada sajjanandadata purari |

Chidananda sandoha mohaphari

Praseeda praseeda Prabho manmathari || 6 ||

O Lord! You are attributeless, auspicious and destroyer of
one cycle of the four Ages (Satya, Treta, Dwapar and Kaliyug).
You are always a source of delight to noble persons! It was
you, who destroyed Tripurasur, the demon. You dispel all
infatuation and you are the Supreme Lord. O Enemy of
Kamdeva, be kind to me and be propitiated.

Na yavad Umanath padar vindam

Bhajuntih loke pare va naranam |

Na tavatsukham shanti santapnasham

Praseeda Prabho sarva bhootadhivasam || 7 ||

Not until human beings adore the feet of the Spouse of
Uma (Parvati), they get peace and happiness either in this
world or the next, not their afflictions end. O Ultimate Abode
of all that is mortal, O Lord Shiv! Be kind to me and be
propitiated.

Na janami yogam japam naiva poojam

Natoaham sada sarvada Shambhu tubhyam |

Jara janma dukkhogh tatapyamanam

Prabho pahi apannamameesh Shambho || 8 ||

O Lord! O Shambhu! O God! I do not know anything
about Yoga, jap and ritual worship. O Lord, I only bow to you.
To me, afflicted by age, decay and other woes of this mortal
world, kindly grant me redemption from these and protect me.

4. श्री मृत्युञ्जय स्तोत्रम्

रत्नसानुशरासनं रजताद्रिश्रृंगनिकेतनं
शिञ्जिनीकृत पन्नगेश्वर मच्युता नल सायकम्।
क्षिप्रदग्धपुरजयं त्रिदशाल यैरभि वन्दितं
चन्द्रशेखर माश्रये मन किं करिष्यति वै यम: ।। 1 ।।

कैलाश शिखर पर जिनका निवास गृह है, जिन्होंने मेरुगिरि का धनुष, नागराज वासुकि की प्रज्यञ्चा और भगवान विष्णु को अग्निमय बाण बना कर तत्काल ही दैत्यों के तीनों पुरों को दग्ध कर डाला था; सम्पूर्ण देवता जिनके चरणों की वन्दना करते हैं – उन भगवान चन्द्रशेखर की मैं शरण लेता हूँ। यमराज मेरा क्या कर लेगा?

पञ्च पादप पुष्प गन्धि पदाम्बुजद्वय शाभितं
भाल लोचन जात पावक दग्ध मन्मथ विग्रहम्।
भस्मदिग्ध कलेवरं भवनाशिनं भव भव्ययं
चन्द्रशेखर माश्रये यम किं करिष्यति वै यम: ।। 2 ।।

मन्दार, पारिजात, संतान, कल्पवृक्ष और हरिचन्दन इन पाँच दिव्य वृक्षों के पुष्पों से सुगन्धित युगल चरण-कल जिनकी शोभा बढ़ाते हैं, जिन्होंने अपने ललाटवर्ती नेत्र से प्रकट हुई आग की ज्वाला में कामदेव के शरीर को भस्म कर डाला था; जिनका श्री विग्रह सदा भस्म से विभूषित रहता है; जो भव-सबकी उत्पत्ति के कारण होते हुए भी भी भव-संसार के नाशक हैं तथा जिनका कभी विनाश नहीं होता-उन भगवान चन्द्रशेखर की मैं शरण लेता हूँ। यमराज मेरा क्या कर लेगा?

4. Shree Mrityunjaya Strotra
(A Hymn for Defying Eeath)

Ratnasanusharasanam rajatadrishringaniketam

Shinjinikrita pannageshwar machyutanal sayakam |

Kshipradagdhapuratrayam Tridashal yerabhi vandita

Chandrashekhar mashraye mum kim karishyati

vai yamah || 1 ||

He whose home is at the Mount Kailash, who had incin-erated the three cities of the Demons by using Meru Mount as the bow, the serpent king Vasuki as the bow-string and Lord Vishnu as the Fiery Arrow; who is adored by all the gods-I seek shelter in such Lord Chandrashekhar. What damage the death-god can infict upon me?

Pancha padapushpa gandhi padambuja dwaya shobhitam

Bhallochan jat pavak dagdha manmath vigraham |

Bhasmadigdha Kalevaram bhavaashinam bhav mavyayam

Chandrashekar mashraye mum kim karishyati

vai yamah || 2 ||

The five flowers: Mandar, Parijata, Santan, Kalpavriksha and Harichandan that are used in the worship of whose feet, whose forhead had beamed a fire to incinerate the body of Kamdeva; whose body is ever smeared with the ash; who destroys this world but himself is ever indestructible-I seek shelter in such Lord Chandrashekhar. What damage the death-god can inflict upon me?

मत्तवारण मुख्य चर्म कृतो तरीय मनोहरं
पङ्कजासन पद्मलोचन पूजिता ङिघ्रसरोरुहम्।
देव सिद्धत तरंगिणीकर सिक्त शीत जटाधरं
चन्द्रशेखर माश्रये मम किं करिष्यति वै यम: ।। 3 ।।

जो मतवाले गजराज के मुख्य चर्म की चादर ओढ़े परम मनोहर जान पड़ते हैं; ब्रह्मा और विष्णु भी जिनके चरण-कमलों की पूजा करते हैं तथा जो देवताओं और सिद्धों की नदी गंगा की तरंगों से भीगी हुई शीतल जटा धारण करते हैं, उन भगवान चन्द्रशेखर की मैं शरण लेता हूँ। यमराज मेरा क्या कर लेगा?

कुण्डलीकृत कुण्डलीश्वर कुण्डलं वृषवाहनं
नारदादि मुनीश्वरस्तुत वैभवं भुवनेश्वरम्।
अन्धकान्तकमाश्रितामर पादपं शमनान्तकं
चन्द्रशेखर माश्रये मय किं करिष्यति वै यम: ।। 4 ।।

कुण्डली मारे हुए सर्पराज जिनके कानों में कुण्डल का काम देते हैं, जो वृषभ की सवारी करते हैं, नारद आदि मुनीश्वर जिनके वैभव की स्तुति करते हैं, जो समस्त भुवनों के स्वामी, अन्धकासुर का नाश करने वाले, आश्रितों के लिए कल्पवृक्ष के समान और यमराज को भी शान्त करने वाले हैं, उन भगवान चन्द्रशेखर मी मैं शरण लेता हूँ। यमराज मेरा क्या कर लेगा?

यक्षराज सखं भगाक्षिहरं भुजङ्गविभूषण
शैलराजसुता परिष्कृत चारुवाम कलेवरम्।
क्ष्वेड नीलगलं परश्वधधारिणं मृण धारिणं
चन्द्रशेखर माश्रये मम किं करिष्यति वै यम: ।। 5 ।।

जो पक्षराज कुबेर के सखा, भग देवता की आँख फोड़ने वाले और सर्पों के आभूषण धारण करने वाले हैं, जिनके श्री विग्रह के सुन्दर वाम

Mattavaranmukhyacharma krittottariya manoharam

Pankajasana padmalochan poojitan grhisaroruham |

Dev siddhat ranginikar sikta sheeta jatadharam

Chandrashekhar mashraye mum kim karishyati vai yamah || 3 ||

He who looks elegant in donning the skin of a 'must'elephant; whose feet are ever adored by Brahma and Vishnu; whose tendril hair are kept wet by the divine and holy river Ganga-I seek shelter in such Lord Chandrashekhar. What damage can the death-god inflict upon me?

Kundalikrita kundaleeshwar kundalam Vrishavahanam

Naradadimuneeshwarstuta vaibhavam Bhuvneshwaram |

Andhakantakmashritamar padapam Shamanantakam

Chandrashekhar mashraye mum kim karishyati vai yamah || 4 ||

The coils of the serpent-lord act as his earrings, who rides a bull; all the sages like Narad, etc. ever adore whose glory; who rules the entire universe; the destroyer of the demon Andhak; who is like the Kalpavriksha (the divine tree fulfilling all desire) to his devotees and who can even quell the manouvres of Yamraj-I seek shelter in such Lord Chandrashekhar. What damage can the death-god inflict upon me?

Yaksharaj sakham bhagakshiharam bhujang vibhushanam

Shailrajsuta parishkrita charuvam kalevaram |

Kshvedaneela galam parashvadhdharinam mriga dharinam

Chandrashekhar mashraye mum kim karishyati vai yamah || 5 ||

He who is Yaksha Lord Kuber's friend, who pierced the eye of the god named Bhag, who carries the serpents as his orna-

भाग को गिरिराज किशोरी उमा ने सुशोभित कर रखा है; कालकूट विष पीने के कारण जिनका कण्ठभाग नीले रंग का दिखाई देता है; जो एक हाथ में फरसा और दूसरे में मृग लिए रहते हैं, उन भगवान चन्द्रशेखर की मैं शरण लेता हूँ। यमराज मेरा क्या कर लेगा?

भेषजं भवरोगिणाम् खिला पदाम पहारिणं
दक्ष यज्ञविनाशनं त्रिगुणात्मकं त्रिविलोचनम्।
मुक्ति मुक्ति फलप्रदम् निखिलाघ संघ निवर्हणं
चन्द्रशेखर माश्रये मम किं करिष्यति वै यमः।। 6 ।।

जो जन्म मरण के रोग से ग्रस्त पुरुषों के लिए औषधि रुप है, समस्त आपत्तियों का निवारण और दक्ष-यज्ञ का विनाश करने वाले हैं, सत्त्व आदि तीनों गुण जिनके स्वरुप हैं, जो तीन नेत्र धारण करते, भोग और मोक्षरुपी फल देते तथा सम्पूर्ण पापराशि का संहार करते हैं, उन भगवान चन्द्रशेखर की मैं शरण लेता हूँ। यमराज मेरा क्या कर लेगा?

भक्त वत्सल मर्चतां निधिमक्षयं हरिदम्बरं
सर्वभूतपतिं परात्परमप्रमेय मनूप मम।
भूमिवारिन भो हुताशन सोम पालित स्वाकृतिं
चन्द्रशेखर माश्रये मम किं करिष्यति वै यमः।। 7 ।।

जो भक्तों पर दया करने वाले हैं, अपनी पूजा करने वाले मनुष्यों के लिए अक्षय निधि होते हुए भी जो स्वयं दिगम्बर रहते हैं, जो सब भूतों के स्वामी, परात्पर, अप्रमेय और उपमारहित हैं, पृथ्वी, जल, आकाश, अग्नि और चन्द्रमा के द्वारा जिनका श्री विग्रह सुरक्षित है, उन भगवान चन्द्रशेखर की मैं शरण लेता हूँ। यमराज मेरा क्या कर लेगा?

ments; on whose left side sits the daughters of the Mountain (Parvati); whose neck has become blue by his imbibing the poision Kaalkoota, who weilds an axe in one hand and a deer in the other-I seek shelter in such Lord Chandrashekhar. What damage can death-god inflict upon me?

Bheshajam bhavaroginam khila padam paharinam

Daksha yagyavinashanam trigunatmakam trilochanam ।

Bhukti bhukti phalpradam nikhilaghasangh nibarhamam

Chandrashekhar mashraye mum kim karishyati vai yamah ।। 6 ।।

He who is the sure remedy for all those afflicted by the diseases of age and mortality; who is the destroyer of the Daksha-Sacrifice and all troubles; in whom repose all the three attributes of the world; who has three eyes; who rewards all enjoyments and eventually the Moksha (soul-salvation)-I seek shelter in such Lord Chandrashekhar. What damage can death god inflict upon me?

Bhakta vatsal marchatam nidhimakshyam haridambaram

Sarvabhootpatim paratparmaprameyamanoopamam ।

Bhoomivarina bho hutashan som-palit swakritim

Chandrashekhar mashraye mum kim karishyati vai yamah ।। 7 ।।

He who is kind to hs devotees; who is infinitely resourceful for his devotees but himself remains unclad; who is Lord of all mortal beings, incomparable and unfathomable; whose form is protected by the earth, water, sky, fire and the moon-I seek shelter in such Lord Chandrashekhar. What damage can the death-god inflict upon me?

विश्वसृष्टि विधायनं पुनरेव पालनतत्परं
संहरन्तमथ प्रपञ्चम शेष लोक निवासिनम्।
क्रीड यन्तमहर्निश गणनाथ यूथ समा वृतं
चन्द्रशेखर माश्रये मम किं करिष्यति वै यम:।। 8 ।।

जो ब्रह्मारूप से सम्पूर्ण विश्व की सृष्टि करते, फिर विष्णुरूप से सबके पालन में संलग्न रहते और अंत में सारे प्रपंच का संहार करते हैं; सम्पूर्ण लोकों में जिनका निवास है तथा जो गणेश जी के पार्षदों से घिर कर दिन-रात भाँति-भाँति के खेल किया करते हैं, उन भगवान चन्द्रशेखर की मैं शरण लेता हूँ। यमराज मेरा क्या कर लेगा?

रुद्रं पशुपतिं स्थाणु नीलकण्ठ मुमापतिम्।
नमामि शिरसा देव किं नो मृत्यु: करिष्यति।। 9 ।।

'रु' अर्थात् दु:ख को दूर करने के कारण जिन्हें रुद्र कहते हैं, जो जीवरुपी पशुओं का पालन करने से पशुपति, स्थिर होने से स्थाणु, गले में नीला चिन्ह धारण करने से नीलकण्ठ और भगवती उमा के पति होने से उमापति नाम धारण करते हैं, उन भगवान शिव को मैं मस्तक झुका कर प्रणाम करता हूँ। मृत्यु मेरा क्या कर लेगी।

कालकण्ठं कलामूर्तिं कालाग्नि कालनाशनामृ।
नमामि शिरसा देवं किं नो मृत्यु करिष्यति।। 10 ।।

जिसके गले में काला (गहन-नील) दाग है, जो कला मूर्ति, कालाग्निस्वरुप और काल के नाशक हैं, उन भगवान शिव को मैं मस्तक झुका कर प्रणाम करता हूँ। मृत्यु मेरा क्या कर लेगी?

Vishwashrishthi vidhayanam punreva palantatparam
Samharantmath prapancham shesh lok niwasinam |
Kreeda yantimaharnisham gananath yooth sama vratam
Chandrashekhar mashraye mum kim karashyati vai yamah || 8 ||

He who creates the world in the form of Brahma, preserves
it in the form of Vishnu and then destroys the whole creation;
who dwells in all the realms; who, surrounded by the henchmen of Lord Ganesh amuses himself by a variety of plays - I
seek shelter in such Lord Chandrashekhar. What damage can
the death god inlfict upon me?

Rudram pashupatim sthanu neelkanthmumapatim |
Namami Shirsa Devam kim no mrityu karishyati || 9 ||

He who is called Rudra because he gets us redemption
from 'Ru' (meaning woes); called Pashupati because he nour-
ishes all animal species: called Sthanu because he is stable;
called Neelkantha because of the poison He carries in his
throat; called Umapati because of His being the Espouse of
Uma (Parvati) - I bow in reverence to such Lord Shiv. What
damage can death inflict upon me?

Kalakantham kalamoortim kalagni kalnashanam |
Namami Shirsa Devam kim no mrityu karishyati || 10 ||

He who has a dark-patch upon his throat; who is the veri-
table form of all art; whose appearance is dreadful like the Fire
of Death; who is the Destroyer of Time—I bow to such Lord
Shiv, in utter reverence. What damage can death inflict upon
me?

नीलकण्ठं विरूपाक्षं निर्मलं निरुपद्रवम्।

नमामि शिरसा देवं किं नो मृत्यु करिष्यति।। 11।।

जिनका कण्ठ नील है और नेत्र विकराल होते हुए भी अत्यंत निर्मल और उपद्रव रहित (शांत) हैं, उन भगवान् शिव को मैं मस्तक झुका कर प्रणाम करता हूँ। मृत्यु मेरा क्या कर लेगी?

वाम देव महादेव लोकनाथं जगद्गुरुम्।

नमामि शिरसा देवं किं नो मृत्युः करिष्यति।। 12।।

जो वामदेव, महादेव, विश्वनाथ और जगद्गुरु नाम धारण करते हैं, उन भगवान शिव को मैं मस्तक झुकाकर प्रणाम करता हूँ। मृत्यु मेरा क्या कर लेगी?

देव देवं जगन्नाथं देवेशमृषभध्वजम्।

नमामि शिरसा देवं किं नो मृत्युः करिष्यति।। 13।।

जो देवताओं के भी आराध्य देव, जगत के स्वामी और देवताओं पर शासन करने वाले हैं, जिनकी ध्वजा पर वृषभ का चिन्ह बना हुआ है, उन भगवान शिव को मैं मस्तक झुका कर प्रणाम करता हूँ। मृत्यु मेरा क्या कर लेगी?

अनन्तमव्ययं शान्तमक्षमालाधरं हरम्।

नमामि शिरसा देवं किं नो मृत्युः करिष्यति।। 14।।

जो अनन्त, अविकारी, शान्त, रुद्राक्षमालाधारी और सब दुःखों को हरने वाले हैं, उन भगवान् शिव को मैं मस्तक झुका कर प्रणाम करता हूँ। मृत्यु मेरा क्या कर लेगी?

Neelkantham viroopaksham nirmalam nirupadravam |
Namami Shirsa Devam kim no mrityu karishyati || 11 ||

He whose throat is blue and the eyes are dreadful yet
totally guileless and steady - I bow in utter reverence to such
Lord Shiv. What damage can death inflict upon me?

Vamdevam Mahadevam Loknatham Jagatgurum |
Namami Shirsa Devam kim no mrityu karishyati || 12 ||

He who is known as Vam Deva, Mahadeva, Vishwanath
and Jagat guru - I bow in reverence to such Lord Shiv. What
damage can death inflict upon me?

Devdevam jagannatham deveshmrishabhadhwajam |
Namami Shirsa Devam kim no mritym karishyati || 13 ||

He who is the chosen Deity of even th gods, the Master of
this World and the Divine Ruler; who has the bull symbol
upon his flag - I bow in reverence to such Lord Shiv. What
damage can death inflict upon me?

Anantamavyam shantmakshamaladharam haram |
Namami Shirsa Devam kim no mritya karashyati || 14 ||

He who is Infinite, Blemishless, Quit, wearing a Rudraksha-
Mala (Lace of Utra Swam Beads); and who ends all woes—I
bow to such Lord Shiv in reverence. What damage can death
inflict upon me?

आनन्दं परमं नित्यं कैवल्य पदकारणम्।
नमामि शिरसा देवं किं नो मृत्यु करिष्यति।। 15।।

जो परमानन्द-स्वरूप, नित्य एवं कैवल्यपद-मोक्ष प्राप्ति के कारण हैं, उन भगवान शिव को मै। मस्तक झुका कर प्रणाम करता हूँ। मृत्यु मेरा क्या कर लेगी?

स्वर्गापवर्गदातारं सृष्टि स्थित्यन्त कारिणम्।
नमामि शिरसा देवं किं नो मृत्यु: करिष्यति।। 16।।

जो स्वर्ग और मोक्ष के दाता तथा सृष्टि, पालन और संहार के कर्ता हैं, उन भगवान शिव को मैं मस्तक झुका कर प्रणाम करता हूँ। मृत्यु मेरा क्या कर लेगी?

Anandam param nityam kaivalya padkaranam |

Namami Shirsa Devam kim no mrityu karishyati || 15 ||

Who is Supreme God, Omnipresent, and the chief cause of getting Moksha (who grants Moksha) - I bow to such Lord Shiv in reverence. What damage can death inflict upon me?

Swargapavargadataram shrishti sthityan karinam |

Namami Shirsa Devam kim no mrityu karishyati || 16 ||

He who is the Bestower of Heaven and Moksha; the Creator, Preserver and Destroyer of the entire Creation - I bow to such Lord Shiv in reverence. What damage can death inflict upon me?

5. श्री शिव चालीसा

जय गनेस गिरिजा सुवन, मंगल मूल सुजान ।
कहति 'अयोध्यादास' तुम देउ अभय वरदान ।।

मैं गिरिराज के पुत्र श्री गणेश की जय-जयकार करता हूँ जो
अत्यधिक ज्ञानी और समस्त मंगलां के मूल (जड़) हैं । (अयोध्यादास कहते
हैं) कि हे गणेश जी, आप मुझे अभय होने का वरदान दें ।

जय गिरिजापति दीन दयाला
सदा करत संतन प्रति पाला । 1 ।

मैं गिरिजापति श्री शंकर की जय बोलता हूँ जो सदा दीनों पर दया
करते हैं और अपने भक्तों (संत जनों) की सदैव रक्षा करते हैं!

भाल चन्द्रमा सोहति नीके
कानन कुण्डल नागफनी के । 2 ।

जिनके मस्तक पर चन्द्रमा सुशोभित है और कानों में कुण्डल की
जगह नाग फन लपेटे बैठे हैं!

अंग गौर शिर गंग बनाई
मुण्ड माल तन क्षार लगाई । 3 ।

उनके गोरे अंग हैं और सिर पर देव नदी गंगा विराजमान है ।
(गले में) मुण्डों की माला है और तन पर भभूति लगी है ।

5. Shree Shiv Chalisa

Jai Ganes Girija suvan, mangal mool sujan I
Kahati 'Ayodhyadas' tum, deu abhaya vardan II

I raise victory-slogans in the name of Shree Ganesh ji, the son of Mother Girija, who is supremely wise and the origin of all auspicious happenings. (Ayodhyadas says): O Lord Ganesh! please grant me a boon of safety and security.

Jai Girijapati deem dayala I
Sada karat Santan pratipala II   1 II

Hail Shree Shankar, the espouse of Mountain's daughter Girija, who is ever kind to the distressed and deprived and always protects his devotees.

Bhal Chandrama sohati neeke I
Kanan kundal nag phani ke II   2 II

He has the moon placed upon his forehead and in his ears, instead of rings, the serpents hand coiling around.

Ang gaur shiv ganga banai I
Mundamal tan kshar lagai II   3 II

He is fair-complexioned with the divine river reposing in his crown. In the neck there is a necklace of hacked off heads and his body is smeared with ash.

वस्त्र खाल बाघम्बर सोहे
छवि को देख नाग-मुनि मोहे। 4 ।

वे वस्त्र की जगह बाघ की खाल धारण किए हैं। उनकी मनोहारी छवि को देख मनुष्य क्या नाग और मुनिगण भी मोहित हो जाते हैं।

मैना मातु की प्रिय दुलारी
बाम अंग राजत शिव प्यारी। 5 ।

मैना माता की प्रिय दुलारी (पार्वती) उनके (भगवान शिव के) बाएं अंग पर विराजमान हैं। वे शिव को अत्यंत प्यारी हैं।

कर में सोह त्रिशूल अतिभारी
करहिं सदा शत्रुन संहारी। 6 ।

उनके हाथ में त्रिशूल विराजमान है जो सदा शत्रुओं का संहार करता रहता है।

नन्दि गनेश सोह तहँ कैसे
'मानस' मध्य कमल हों जैसे। 7 ।

उनके साथ नन्दी और गणेश ऐसे शोभा पा रहे हैं, मानों मानसरोवर में कमल खिल रहे हों।

कार्तिक श्याम और गण राऊ
या छवि बरनत बने न काऊ। 8 ।

उनके साथ श्यामवर्ण कार्तिक (कार्तिकेय) तथा अन्य गणों के सरदार (गणेश) हैं। इस छवि का वर्णन करने में कोई समर्थ नहीं है।

Vastra khal Baghambar sohe |

Chhavi ko dekh nag-muni mohe || 4 ||

Instead of normal clothes he has the skin of panther tied round his waist. Looking at his charming view, let alone humans, even the serpents and high sages get enchanted.

Maina Matu ki priya dulari |

Bam ang rajat Shiv pyari || 5 ||

The beloved daughter (Parvati) of Maina mother is sitting in his lap on the left hand side. She is supremely dear to Lord Shiv.

Kar men soha-trishool ati bhari |

Karahi sada shatrun samhari || 6 ||

He carries a heavy trident in his hand which ever slays the enemy-host.

Nandi Ganesh soh tanha kaise |

'Manas' madhya kamal hon jaise || 7 ||

With him are reposed Nandi (the bull) and Ganesh, so enchantingly as though they are lotus flowers blooming in the lake Mansarovar.

Kartik Shyam aur gana rauo |

Ya chhavi barnat bane na kauo || 8 ||

He has with him dark-complexioned Kartika (Kartikeya) and other chieftain (Ganesh). No one can be capable to describe the full spectacle.

देवनि जब ही आइ पुकारा
तबहिं दुःख प्रभु आप निवारा। 9 ।

जब-जब भी देवताओं पर विपत्ति पड़ी है तब वे आपकी शरण में आए और प्रभु आपने ही उनके दुख का निवारण किया है।

कीन उपद्रव तारक मारी
देवनि सब मिलि तुम्हहिं पुकारी। 10 ।

जब तारकासुर ने भारी उपद्रव किया और देवताओं को त्रस्त किया तो उन्होंने आपको की पुकारा था।

तुरत षडानन आप पठायौ
लव निमेष महि मार गिरायौ। 11 ।

तब तुरंत आपने सडानन (छह मुखों वाले कार्तिकेय) को भेजा जिन्होंने क्षण मात्र में उस असुर को मार गिराया।

आप जलंधर असुर संहारा
सुयश तुम्हार विदित संसारा। 12 ।

आपने जलंधर नामक असुर का भी वध किया था। आपकी कीर्ति समस्त संसार जानता है।

त्रिपुरासुर संग युद्ध मचाई
सबहिं कृपा कर लीन बचाई। 13 ।

त्रिपुरासुर के साथ युद्ध कर आपने उसका संहार कर सब पर कृपा की और देवों को बचा लिया।

Devan jab hee aai pukara |

Tabahin dukh prabhu ap nivara || 9 ||

Whenever the celestials faced problems they invariably sought your shelter, Lord! And then you always provided succour to them.

Keen upadrava Tarak bhari |

Devan sab mili tumahi pukari || 10 ||

When the terrible demon Tarak wrought havoc and distressed the gods, they had sought your help only.

Turat Shadanan ap pathayo |

Luv nimesh mahi mar girayo || 11 ||

Then you had immediately despatched the six faced (Kartikeya) who trounced the demon in no time.

Ap Jullandhar asur sanhara |

Suyash tumhar vidit sansara || 12 ||

You also slayed the demon named Jullandhar. Your glory is well-known to the world.

Tripurasur sang yuddha machayi |

Sabahin kripa kari leen bachayi || 13 ||

Fighting with the Demon Tripurasur, you had slayed him and gracefully saved the gods.

कीन्हा तप भागीरथ मारी
पुरहि प्रतिज्ञा तासु पुरारी। 14।

राजा भागीरथ ने भारी तप किया था (गंगा को लाने हेतु) और आपने प्रसन्न होकर उनकी तपस्या पूरी करवा दी थी। (भागीरथ ने गंगा से प्रार्थना की थी पृथ्वी पर आने के लिए। गंगा ने प्रसन्न होकर पृथ्वी पर आना तो स्वीकार किया था परन्तु यह भी कहा कि उनका वेग पृथ्वी पर कोई सहन नहीं कर सकता। कहीं ऐसा न हो कि वह पृथ्वी फोड़कर सीधी पाताल ही चली जाएं स्वर्ग से। इसलिए भगीरथ ने भगवान शिव की आराधना की कि वह पृथ्वी पर गंगा के वेग को कम कर दें। शिव जी ने गंगा के इस दर्प को भंग करने के लिए न सिर्फ गंगा को अपनी जटाओं में ही समा लिया, वरन् गंगा की गति भी रुक गई थी। तब भागीरथ की पुन: प्रार्थना करने पर ही उनको बाहर छोड़ा था। इसीलिए आज तक गंगा शिव की जटाओं से निकलती ही दर्शित की जाती हैं।)

दर्प छोड़ गंगा तब आई
सेवक अस्तुति करत सदाई। 15।

तब गंगा अपना दर्प छोड़ पृथ्वी पर आई थी। इसीलिए आपके सेवक सदा आपकी स्तुति करते हैं।

वेद नाम महिमा तब गाई
अकथ अनादि भेद न हिं पाई। 16।

वेदों में आपकी महती महिमा वर्णित है परन्तु वह इतनी अधिक है कि कही नहीं जा सकती। आपकी अनादि महिमा का भेद (या अना) पाना असंभव है

Keenha tap Bhagirath bhari |

Purahi pratigya tasu purari | | 14 | |

King Bhagirath had performed a rigorous penance (for bringing down the Ganga) and by your grace you made his mission a success. (Bhagirath had requested the celestial river Ganga to come down to the earth. The river had conceded to the request but said that no one could withstand her cascading down to earth. Lest she might break through the earth and sink down to the Patal lok (the nether worlds)! Then Bhagirath had again sought Lord Shiv's help to bear the thurst of the river Ganga coming down. To browbeat Ganga's this arrogance, Shiv ji made her lose her way in his tendril locks. Hence still the Ganga is shown coming out of Shivji's locks from which she eventually emerged by the Lord's grace.

Darpa chhod Ganga tab ayee |

Sewak astuti karat sadaee | | 15 | |

Then, brow beaten, Ganga, had to come to the earth. That is why your devotees always sing in your praise.

Ved nam mahima tav gayee |

Akath Anadi bhed nahin payee | | 16 | |

The Vedas had tried to describe your glory but it is too great to be effable. It is impossible to fathom your full glory.

प्रगटी उदधि मन्थन ते ज्वाला

जरे सुरासुर भए बिहाला। 17 ।

समुद्र-मन्थन से ऐसी भयानक विष-ज्वाल निकली कि उसने सिन्धु-मन्थन करने वाले देवता तथा असुरों को बेहाल कर दिया था।

महादेव तब करी सहाई

नीलकंठ तब नाम धराई। 18 ।

तब हे महादेव आपने उनकी सहायता की (और विष कंठ में धारण कर लिया)। तभी से आपका नाम नील कंठ हो गया।

पूजन रामचन्द्र जब कीन्हा

लंका जीत विभीषण दीन्हा। 19 ।

जब रामचन्द्र जी ने आपका पूजन किया तो आपकी कृपा से उन्होंने लंका पर विजय प्राप्त की और लंका जीत कर विभीषण को दे दी।

सहस कमल अरपनिह विचारी

कीन्ह परीक्षा तबहि पुरारी। 20 ।

तब रामचन्द्र जी ने सहस्त्र कमल अर्पित कर भगवान शंकर की पूजा करने का विचार किया। तब उनकी आस्था की दृढ़ता जाँचने हेतु पुरारी (भगवान शंकर) ने उनकी परीक्षा ली।

Pragati udadhi manthan te jwala |
Jare surasur bhaye bihala | | 17 | |

The Sea-Churning had produced such a dreadful poison-
flame that its heat and toxic effect severely distressed the gods
and the demons both.

Mahadeva tab kari sahayee |
Neelkantha tuv nam dharayee | | 18 | |

Then O Great, Lord, you came to their rescue and drank
that poison to let it remain deposited in your throat, which
caused it to go blue. Hence your name Blue Throated or Neel-
Kanth.

Poojan Ramchandra jab keenha |
Lanka jeet Vibhishan deenha | | 19 | |

When Lord Rama worshipped you, you granted him the
boon of victory. Then he won Lanka and later made Vibhishan
its king.

Sahas kamal arpanahi vichari |
Keenha pareeksha tabahi purari | | 20 | |

(During the worship) Lord Rama decided to offer you a
thousand lotus flowers. Then to assess his firmness in the faith,
you had tested him.

एक कमल प्रभु राखेऊ गोई

कमल नयन पूजन चहिं सोई । 21 ।

और शंकर जी! आपने उनमें से एक कमल तब छुपा लिया था। फिर उस कमल के बदले जब रामचन्द्र जी ने अपना नयन-कमल जैसा-दान करने की चेष्टा की तो.....

कठिन भक्ति देखी प्रभु शंकर

भए प्रसन्न देय इच्छितवर । 22 ।

भगवान शंकर उनकी अटल भक्ति से प्रसन्न हो गए और उन्हें इच्छित वरदान दे दिया।

जय-जय-जय अनन्त अविनासी

करत कृपा सबके घट वासी । 23 ।

हे अनन्त, हे अवनाशी प्रभु। आपकी जय हो जय.....हो.....जय हो। आप अंर्तयामी हैं और सब पर कृपा करते हैं।

दुष्ट सकल मोहि नित्य सतावें

भ्रमित रहे मन चैन न आवें । 24 ।

सारे दुष्ट जन मुझे सदैव सताया करते हैं। चित्त भ्रमित रहता है और चैन नहीं मिलता है।

त्राहि-त्राहि मैं नाथ पुकारो

यह अवसर मोहि आनि उबारो । 25 ।

इन आपदाओं से त्रस्त होकर मैंने नाथ (भगवान शंकर) को पुकरा है....हे प्रभु.....इस कठिन अवसर पर आकर मुझे उबारो!

Ek kamal Prabhu rakheu goyee |

Kamal nayan poojan chahin soyee | | 21 | |

And, O Lord Shankar! You had hidden one of the flowers. Not finding it, when Lord Ramam tried to substitute his eye— also like lotus—for it,....

Kathin bhakti dekhi Prabhu Shankar |

Bhaye prasanna deya icchhit var | | 22 | |

Lord Shankar! You were propitiated by his devoutness and granted him (Lord Rama) the desired boom. Then only he could slay Ravan and win Lanka.

Jai-Jai-Jai ananta avinasi |

Karat kripa sab ke ghatvasi | | 23 | |

O Infinite! O Indestructible Lord! Victory to thee .... to thee! You are omniscient and shower your grace on every body.

Dushta sakal mohi nitya satavan |

Bharmita rahe man chain na aven | | 24 | |

I am always troubled by the wicked persons who ever torment me. This makes me sorely distressed with no peace of mind.

Trahi-trahi main nath pukaro |

Yeh avasar mohi ani ubaro | | 25 | |

Getting distressed, I pray Lord Shankar to provide me succour .... O Lord! Help me in this tormenting hour.

लाइ त्रिशूल शत्रुन को मारौ
संकट से मोहि आनि उबारौ। 26।

आप अपने त्रिशूल द्वारा शत्रुओं को मार कर मुझे इस संकट से
छुटकारा प्रदान करें।

माता-पिता भ्रात सब होई
संकट में पूछत नहिं कोई। 27।

वैसे तो मेरे माता-पिता-भाई इत्यादि सब ही हैं किन्तु संकट में मुझे
कोई नहीं पूछता (अर्थात् कोई मुझे पहिचानता भी नहीं, सहायता करना
तो दूर की बात है)।

स्वामी एकहि आस तुम्हारी
आइ हरहु सब संकट भारी। 28।

हे प्रभु! मेरी तो एक आस आपसे ही है! हे स्वामी! आप आकर मेरा
यह भारी संकट दूर करें।

धन निर्धन को देत सदाई
आरत जन की पीर मिटाई। 29।

आप सदैव आर्तजनों की पीड़ा हरते हैं और भक्त की मनोकामना
पूर्ण करते हैं.....आप जिस पर जिसका अभाव हो उसकी पूर्ति करते हैं.
.......जैसे निर्धन को धन आप ही देते हैं।

अस्तुति केहि विधि करहु तुम्हारी
शंभुनाथ अब टेक हमारी। 30।

हे शिव शंभो.....हमारी विनती सुनिए.....हमें कष्टों से त्राण दीजिए.
.....और मैं नहीं जानता कि आपकी स्तुति हम कैसे करें।

Lai trishool shatrun ko marau l

Sankat se mohi ani Ubarau l l   26 l l

Come with you Trident and slay my enemies to redeem
me from this tortue.

Mata-pita bhrat sab hoi l

Sankat men poonchat nahi koi l l   27 l l

Although I have my parents, brothers, etc., yet in distress
no body comes for my resuce. I have no hope from any other
quarter.

Swami ekahi aas tumhari l

Ai harahu sab sankat bhari l l   28 l l

O Lord! You are my only hope. O Master! Please come to
give me help in this distressing hour.

Dhan nirdhan kon det sadaee l

Arat jan ki peer mitaee l l   29 l l

You always provide succour to the distressed and ever
fulfils the wish of your devotees. You end their privation by
providing the thing they desiderate for. Like you grant riches
to the pauper.

Astuti kehi vidhi karahu tumhari l

Shambhunath ab tek hamari l l   30 l l

O Lord Shankar! Please hark to my prayer and provide
solace from this distress. I know no other way to seek help
from you, O Lord!

शंकर हो संकट के नाशन
विघ्न विनासन मंगल कारण। 31।

हे शंकर जी! आप मेरे संकट का नाश कीजिए। मेरे विघ्न का विनाश
कर मेरे मंगल का कारण आप बनिए.........अर्थात् मेरे संकट का नाश
कर मेरा कल्याण कीजिए।

योगी यति मुनि ध्यान लगावहिं
शारद नारद शीश नवावहिं। 32।

सारे योगी यती और मुनिजन आपका ही ध्यान लगाते हैं तथा शारदा
(सरस्वती देवी) नारद इत्यादि ऋषिगण आपको ही शीश नवाते हैं।

नमो नमो जय नम: शिवाये
सुर ब्रहमादिक पार न पाए। 33।

मैं ॐ नम: शिवाय का जाप करता हूँ। हे भगवान शिव। आपकी
पूर्ण महिमा तो सुर और ब्रहमा आदि भी नहीं जान पाए हैं।

जो यह पाठ करे मन लाई
ता को होत हैं शंभु सहाई। 34।

जो इस पाठ को मन लगा कर पूरा करेगा उसकी भगवान शंभु
निश्चय ही सहायता करेंगे-इसमें कोई संदेह नहीं!

पुत्र न हो, इच्छा करे कोई
निश्चय शिव प्रसाद से होई। 35।

यदि कोई निस्संतान है और पुत्र प्राप्ति की कामना रखता है तो
शंभु के प्रसाद रूप उसको पुत्र-रत्न की अवश्य प्राप्ति होगी।

Shankar ho sankat ke nashan |

Vighna vinasan mangal karan | | 31 | |

O Lord Shankar! Please end my affliction! Destroying the cause of my trouble, be the root of my happiness and welfare.

Yogi yati muni dhyan lagavahin |

Sharad narad sheesh navavahin | | 32 | |

All the high sages, yogis and adepts always concentrate their mind on Your Visage, Lord! The Goddess of Wisdom Sharada (Saraswati), the sage Narad and other seers ever bow in reverence to you only.

Namo namo jap namah Shivaye |

Sur brahmadik par na paye | | 33 | |

I now chant 'Om Namah Shivaye'! O Lord Shiv, neither gods nor brahma could ever fathom your entire glory.

Jo yeh path kare man layee |

Ta kon hot hain shambhu sahayee | | 34 | |

He who reads this Chalisa with full concentration and devotion shall be definitely helped by Lord Shambhu—there is no doubt about it.

Putra na ho, ichha kare koi |

Nishchaya Shiv prasad se hoi | | 35 | |

If anyone be without any male issue and desirous of getting one, then by the grace of Lord Shambhu he shall definitely get a son.

पंडित त्रयोदशी को लावे
ध्यान पूर्वक होम करावे । 36 ।

भक्त जन को चाहिए कि त्रयोदशी तिथि को पंडित लेकर आवे तथा उससे पूरे ध्यान पूर्वक होम करावे ।

त्रयोदशी व्रत करे हमेशा
तन नहीं ताके रहे कलेशा । 37 ।

जौ त्रयोदशी का सदैव व्रत करता है उसका शरीर और मन निर्मल रहता है तथा उसको क्लेश भी नहीं व्यापता ।

धूप-दीप नैवेद्य चढ़ावहिं
शंकर सनमुख पाठ करावहिं । 38 ।

धूप-दीप नैवेद्य इत्यादि चढ़ाकर शंकर के सामने ध्यान पूर्वक पूजा करनी चाहिए ।

जनम-जनम के पाप नसावहिं
अंतवास शिवपुर में पावहिं । 39 ।

ऐसे भक्त जन के जनम-जनम के पाप मिट जाते हैं औत अंत काल में मृत्योपरांत शिवपुर (काशी या कैलाश पर्वत) में शंकर भगवान के निकट ही निवास रहता है ।

हे शंकर हे आस तुम्हारी
दुख-पीड़ा अब हरहु हमारी । 40 ।

हे भगवान शंकर! हमारी तो एक मात्र आस आप पर ही है । अब हमारी पीड़ा और दुखों का हरण आप ही करें ।

Pandit triyodashi ko lave |

Dhyan poorvak hom karave || 36 ||

The devout (desirous of having his wish fulfilled by Lord Shambhu's grace) must get a priest on the 13th lunar day of the fortnight and with full devotion must have the ritual Yagya performed.

Triyodashi vrita kare hamesha |

Tan nahin take rahe kalesha || 37 ||

He who keeps fast on the thirteenth day of the lumar fortnight, derives peace of the mind and even his body remains free of any affliction.

Dhoop-deep naivedya Chadhavahi |

Shankar sanmukha path karavahi || 38 ||

With incense and lighted lamp and other material, he should worship before the idol of Lord Shankar with full devotion.

Janam-janam ki pap nasavahin |

Antawas Shivpur men pavahin || 39 ||

Such a devotee will have all his sins accruing to him from many births destroyed and he would emerge clean. Then after his death he shall live in the realm of Lord Shiv (in Kashi or Kailash mount) happily.

Hey Shankar hai aas tumhari |

Dukh-peerha ab harahu hamari || 40 ||

O Lord Shankar! You are my only hope! Now please end all my pains and woes and provide me solace.

श्री मच्छङ्कराचार्य कृतो

6. वेदसार शिवस्तवः

पशूनां पतिं पापनाशं परेशं

  गजेन्द्रस्य कृत्तिं वसानं वरेण्यम्।

जटा जूट मध्ये स्फुरद्गांगवारि

  महादेवमेकं स्मरामि स्मरारिम्।। 1।।

जो सम्पूर्ण प्राणियों के रक्षक हैं, पाप का ध्वंस करने वाले हैं, परमेश्वर
हैं, गजराज का चर्म पहने हुए हैं तथा श्रेष्ठ हैं और जिनके जटाजूट में
श्री गंगा जी खेल रही हैं, उन एक मात्र कामारि (काम के शत्रु) श्री
महादेव जी का मैं स्मरण करता हूँ।

महेशं सुरेशं सुरारार्तिं नाशं

  विभुं विश्वनाथं विभत्यङ्गभूषम्।

विरूपाक्षमिन्द्वर्कवह्नित्रिनेत्रं

  सदानन्द मीडे प्रभुं पञ्चवक्त्रम्।। 2।।

चन्द्र सूर्य और अग्नि—तीनों जिनके नेत्र हैं, उन विरूप नयन महेश्वर,
देवेश्वर, देवदुःखदलन, विभु विश्वनाथ, विभूति भूषण, नित्यानंद स्वरुप,
पंचमुख भगवान महादेव की मैं स्तुति करता हूँ।

6. The Essence of Description of Lord Shiv in the Vedas
(Created by Shankarcharya)

Pashoonam patim papnasham paresham

Gajendrasya krittim vasanam varenyam |

Jata joot madhye sphurbhdangvari

Mahadevamekam smrami smrami | | 1 | |

He who is protector of all beings; who is destroyer of all sins; who wears the skin of a large elephant for his clothes; who is exalted and in whose tendril locks playfully flows the river Ganga - I chant his name, Lord Shankar, the enemy of Kamdeva, the lord of love.

Mahesham suresham suraratinasham

Vibhum vishwanatham vibhutyangbhovsham |

Virupakshamindvark vahnitrinetram

Sadananda meede Prabhum panchavaktram | | 2 | |

The sun, the moon and fire are whose three eyes, that Great Lord, Master of gods, the Helper to gods in their hour of distress, the Lord of the World, the Glorious Existence, the Abode of Bliss, the Five-Faced Lord Mahadeva is now hymned by me.

गिरीशं गणेशं गले नीलवर्णं
गवेन्द्राधिरूढं गणातीत रूपम्।
भवं भास्वरं भस्मना भूषिताङ्गम्
भवानी कलत्रं हैं, भजे पञ्चवक्त्रम्।। 3 ।।

जो कैलाशनाथ है, गणनाथ हैं, नीलकण्ठ हैं, बैल पर चढ़े हुए हैं,
अगणित रूप वाले हैं, संसार के आदिकरण हैं प्रकाश स्वरूप हैं, शरीर
में भस्म लगाए हुए हैं और श्री पार्वती जी जिनकी अर्द्धांगिनी हैं, उन
पंचमुख महादेव जी को मैं भजता हूँ।। 3 ।।

शिवाकान्त शम्भो शशाङ्काार्ध मौले
महेशान शूलिन् जटाजूट धारिन्।
त्वमेको जगद् व्यापको विश्वरूप
प्रसीद प्रसीद प्रभो पूर्ण रूपं।। 4 ।।

हे पार्वतजी वल्लभ महादेव! हे चन्द्र शेखर! हे महेश्वर! हे त्रिशूलिन्!
हे जटाजूट धारिन! हे विश्वरूप! हे विश्वरूप! एकमात्र आप ही जगत् में
व्यापक हैं। हे पूर्णरूप प्रभो! प्रसन्न होइए, प्रसन्न होईए!

परामात्मानमेकं जगद्बीज माद्यं
निरीहं निराकार मोङ्कार वेदम्
यतो जायते पाल्यते येन विश्वम्
तमीशं भजे लीयते यत्र विश्वम्।। 5 ।।

जो परमात्मा है, एक हैं, जगत् के आदिकारण हैं, इच्छा रहित हैं
निराकार हैं और प्रणव द्वारा जानने योग्य हैं तथा जिनसे सम्पूर्ण विश्व
की उत्पत्ति और पालन होता है और फिर जिनमें उसका लय हो जजात
है, उन प्रभु को मैं भजता हूँ।। 5 ।।

Girisham Ganesham gale neelvarnam

Gavendradhiroodham ganateet roopam |

Bhavam bhaswaram bhasmna bhooshitangam

Bhavani kalatram bhaje panchavaktram | | 3 | |

He who is the Lord of the Mount Kailash, the Master of his henchmen; who is astride the bull, who has infinite forms; who is the root-cause of this world; the manifestation of Light; who has his body smeared with ash; whose wife is goddess Parvati I—bow to that Five Faced Lord Mahadeva!

Shivakant Shambhoo shashankardhamaule

Maheshan shoolin jatajootdharin |

Tvameko jagadvyapako vishwaroop

Praseeda praseeda Prabho poornaroopam | | 4 | |

O Great Lord, the Espouse of Parvati Ji! O Lord with the moon at his crown! O Weilder of Trident! O Tendril-haired Lord! O Universal Form! With you whole world is instinct! O Complete God! Be pleased, be pleased!

Paratmanmekam jagdweej madhyam

Nireeham nirakar monkar vedyam |

Yato ja yate palyate yen vishwam

Tameesham bhaje leeyate yatra vishwam | | 5 | |

He who is the Supreme Lord, Unique, the root cause of the wordly existence, who is desireless, formless and known only through the inner voice—the Pranava (Omkar); who is the Creator, Preserver and Destroyer of the world—I bow to such Great Shankar.

83

न भूमिर्न चापो न वह्निर्न वायु-
        र्न चाकाशमास्ते न तन्द्रा न निद्रा।
न ग्रीष्मो न शीतं न देशो न वेषो
        न चस्याति मूर्तिस्त्रिमूर्तिं तमीडे।। 6।।

जो न पृथ्वी है, न जल है, न अग्नि है, न वायु है और न आकाश है,
न तन्द्रा है, न निद्रा है न ग्रीष्म है और न शीत है तथा जिसका न कोई
देश है न वेष है, उन मूर्तिहीन त्रिमूर्ति की मैं स्तुति करता हूँ।। 6।।

अजं शाश्वतं कारणं कारणानां
        शिवं केवलं भासकं भासकानाम्।
तुरीयं तम: पारमाद्यन्तहीनं
        प्रपद्ये परं पावनं द्वैतहीनम्।। 7।।

जो अजन्मा है, नित्य है, कारण के भी कारण है, कल्याणरूपी है,
एक हैं, प्रकाशकों के भी प्रकाशक हैं, अवस्था त्रय से भी विलक्षण हैं,
अज्ञान से भी परे है, अनादि और अनन्त है, उन परम पावन अद्वैत स्वरूप
को मैं प्रणाम करता हूँ।। 7।।

नमस्ते नमस्ते विभो विश्वमूर्ते
        नमस्ते नमस्ते चिदानन्दमूर्ते
नमस्ते नमस्ते तपोयोग गम्य
        नमस्ते नमस्ते श्रुतिज्ञान गम्य।। 8।।

हे विश्व मूर्ते! हे विभो! आपको नमस्कार है, नमस्कार है। हे चिदानन्द मूर्ते!
आपको नमस्कार है, नमस्कार है। तप और योग से प्राप्तव्य प्रभो! आपको नमस्कार
है, नमस्कार है हे वेद वेद्य भगवान। आपको नमस्कार है, नमस्कार है!

Na bhoomirna chapo na vahinuru vayu-

rna chakashamaste na tandra na nidra |

Na greeshmo na sheetam na desho na vesho

Na chasyati moortirstrimoortim tameede | | 6 | |

He who is neither the earth, nor water, nor fire, nor wind, nor the sky, nor drowsiness nor sleep, nor the summer, nor winter, nor has any dwelling space nor any guise—I bow to that Formless Trinity and hymn in reverence.

Ajam shashwatam karanam karnaanam

Shivam kewalam bhasakam bhaskaanam |

Tureeyam tamah parmadyantaheenam

Prapadye param pavanam dwetheenam | | 7 | |

He who is unborn, Eternal, the root cause of any cause; who is Auspicious, Unique; the source of All Light; beyond the three stages of the body; far away from ignorance; who has neither the beginning nor end—I bow to that Supremely Pious One Entity!

Namaste Namaste vibho vishwamoorte

Namaste namaste chidanandamoorte |

Namaste namaste tapoyog gamya

Namaste namaste shrutigyan gamya | | 8 | |

O Universal Form! O God! I bow to you handbound! O Manifestation of Eternal Bliss! I bow to you, bow to you! O Lord, attainable only by penance and Yoga! I bow to you, bow to you! O Lord, orisoned by the Vedas! I bow to you again and again in reverence.

प्रभो शूलपाणे विभो विश्वनाथ
        महादेव शम्भो महेश त्रिनेत्र ।
शिवाकान्त शान्त स्मरारे पुरारे
        त्वदन्यो वरेण्यो न मान्यो न गण्यः ।। 9 ।।

हे प्रभो! हे त्रिशूलपाणे! हे विभो! हे विश्वनाथ! हे महादेव! हे शम्भो! हे महेश्वर!
हे त्रिनेत्र! हे पार्वती प्राणवल्लभ! हे शान्त! हे कामारि (काम-शत्रु)। हे त्रिपुरारे!
तुम्हारे अतिरिक्त न कोई श्रेष्ठ है, न माननीय है और न गणनीय है।

शम्भो महेश करुणामय शूलपाणे
        गौरीपते पशुपते पशुपाशनाशिन् ।
काशीपते करुणया जगदेत देक-
        स्त्वं हंसि पासि विदधासि महेश्वरोऽसि ।। 10 ।।

त्वत्तो जगद्भवतिदेव भव स्मरारे
        त्वय्येव तिष्ठति जगन्मृड विश्वनाथ ।
त्वय्येव गच्छति लयं जगदेतदीश
        लिंगात्मकं हर चराचर विश्वरूपिन् ।। 11 ।।

हे शम्भो! हे महेश्वर! हे करुणामय! हे त्रिशूलिन्! हे गौरीपते! हे पशुपते!
हे पशुबन्ध मोचन! हे काशीश्वर! एक तुम्हीं करुणावश इस जगत की उत्पत्ति,
पालन और संहार करते हो; हे कन्दर्पदलन! हे शिव! हे विश्वनाथ! हे ईश्वर!
हे हर! हे चराचर जगद्रूप प्रभो! यह लिंगमय स्वरूप समस्त जगत तुम से ही
उत्पन्न होता है; तुम्हीं में स्थित रहता है और तुम्हीं में लय हो जाता है।

Prabho shoolpane vibho vishwanath
Mahadeva Shambho Mahesh Trinetra |
Shivakant shanta smarare purare
Twadanyo varenyo na manyo na ganyah | | 9 | |

O Lord! O trident Weilder! O God! O Universe's Master! O Mahadeva! O Shambho! O Maheshwar! O with Three Eyes! O spouse of Parvati! O Quite! O Enemy of Kamdeva! O Destroyer of Tripur! No one else is greater, more honourable or countable than You are!

Shambho Mahesh karunamaya shoolpane
Gauripate pashupate pashupashnashinam |
Kashipate karunya jagadeta dek-
Stvam hansi pasi vidadhasi Maheshwrasi | | 10 | |

Tvatoo jagadbhavati deva bhav smaraare
Tvayyeva tishthati jaganmrida vishwanath |
Tvayyeva gachhati layam jagdetadeesha
Lingatmakam har charachar vishwaroopin | | 11 | |

O Shambho! O Maheshwar! O Kind-hearted! O Trident weilder! O spouse of Gauri (Parvati)! O Pashupati! O Release from the animal bondage! O Lord of Kashi! You are the sole cause of this world's coming into existence, its preservation and its eventual dissolution. You are the Sole Lord! O God! O Shankar! O Browbeater of Kamdeva! O Shiva! O Universal Form! O Lord! O Har! O Epitome of carnal contradictions. This world gets births through your symbol, the Linga. You alone preserve and destroy it.!

7. शिव जी की आरती

जय शिव ओंकारा
(प्रभु जय शिव ओंकारा)
ब्रह्मा विष्णु सदाशिव अर्धांगी धारा ।
(ओम् हर-हर-हर-महादेव.....)

एकानन चतुरानन पंचानन राजे
हंसासन गरुडासन वृषवाहन साजे
(ओम् हर-हर-हर-महादेव.....)

दो भुज चारु चर्तुभुज दशमुख अति सोहे
तीनों रुप निरखते त्रिभुवन जन मोहे
(ओम् हर-हर-हर-महादेव.....)

अक्षमाला बनमाला मुण्डमाला धारी
चन्दन मृगमद सोहे, माले शुभकारी
(ओम् हर-हर-हर-महादेव.....)

श्वेताम्बर पीताम्बर बाघम्बर अंगे
ब्रह्मादिक सनकादिक प्रेतादिक संगे
(ओम् हर-हर-हर-महादेव.....)

कर में एक कमण्डल औ' त्रिशूल धर्ता
सुखकारी दुखहारी जग पालन कर्ता
(ओम् हर-हर-हर-महादेव.....)

ब्रह्मा विष्णु सदाशिव जानत अविवेका

7. The Arti of Lord Shiva

Jai Shiv ondara

(Prabhu Jai Shiv Onkara)

Brahma Vishnu Sadashiv ardhangi dhara!

(Om Har-Har-Har-Mahadeva!)

Ekanan Chaturanan panchanan raje

Hansasan Garudasan Vrisha-vahan saje

(Om Har-Har-Har-Mahadeva!)

Do bhuj charu chaturbhuja dashmukha ati sohe

Teenon roop nirakhate tribhuvan jan mohe

(Om Har-Har-Har-Mahadeva!)

Akshamala banmala mundamala dhari

Chandan mrigamad sohe, bhale shubhakari

(Om Har-Har-Har-Mahadeva!)

Shetambar peetambar baghambar ange

Brahmadik sanakadik pretadik sange

(Om Har-Har-Har-Mahadeva!)

Kar men ek kamandal au trishool dharta

Sukhakari, dukhahari jagpalan karta

(Om Har-Har-Har-Mahadeva!)

Brahma Vishnu Sadashiv janat aviveka

प्रणवक्षर में शोभित ये तीनों एका
(ओम् हर-हर-हर-महादेव.....)
त्रिगुण स्वामि की आरति जो कोई नर गावे
कहत 'शिवानन्द स्वामी' वांछति फल पावे
(ओम् हर-हर-हर-महादेव.....)

Pranavakshar men shobhit ye teenon eka
(Om-Har-Har-Har-Mahadeva!)
Triguna Swami ki arti jo koi nar gave
Kahat 'Shivananda Swami' vanchhita phal pave
(Om-Har-Har-Har-Mahadeva!)

❑❑❑

(गोस्वामी तुलसीदास कृत)

8. एक याचना

यस्यांके च विभति भूधर सुता देवा पगा मस्तके
भाले वाल विर्धुगले च गरलं यस्योरसि व्यालराट्
सोऽयं भूति विभूषण: सुरवर: सर्वाधिप: सर्वदा
शर्व: सर्वगत: शिव: शशिनिभ: श्री शंकर: पातुमाम्!

(जिनकी गोद में पार्वती जी, मस्तक पर गंगा जी, भाल पर द्वितीया का चन्द्रमा, कण्ठ में विष और वक्षस्थल पर नागराज सुशोभित हैं, वे भस्म से विभूषित देवों में श्रेष्ठ, सर्वेश्वर, संहारकर्ता, सर्वव्यापक, कल्याण रुप, चन्द्र वर्ण श्री शंकर जी सदा मेरी रक्षा करें।)

8. A Request

Yasyanke cha vibhati bhoodharsuta Devapaga mastake
Bhalebal vidhurugale cha garalam yasyorasi vyalrat
Soayam bhooti-vibhooshanam Suravarah sarvadhipah sarvada
Sharvah sarvagatah Shivah shashinibhah Shee shankarah patumam

[In whose lap reposes the daughter of the Mountains; and whose head carries the divine river (Ganga); in whose throat is depoisted poison; the forhead has the moon of the second day; the chest is bedight with the great serpent; whose body is smeared with the ash, he, the Greatest God and Lord of All, the Destroyer, the Omnipresent, of auspicious form with a body like the shining moon may ever protect me.]

DIAMOND POCKET BOOKS

SELECTED BOOKS FOR ALL

OSHO BOOKS

Medittation : The Art of Ecstasy	100.00
And the Flowers Showered	80.00
The Great Challenge	60.00
Zen and the Art of Enlightnment	100.00
Zen and the Art of Living	100.00
Zen and the Art of Mediation	100.00
Zen : Take it Easy	100.00
I am the Gate	100.00
Psychology of the Esoteric	60.00
Bauls : The Dancing Mystics	30.00
Bauls : The Seekers of the Path	30.00
Bauls : The Mystics of Celebration	30.00
Bauls : The Singing Mystics	30.00
Ecstasy : The Language of Existaence	30.00
Fly Without Wings	30.00
Be Oceanic	30.00
The Greatest Gamble	30.00
Here & Now	30.00
Towards the Unknown	30.00
Vedanta : The Ultimate Truth	30.00
Vedanta : The First Star in the Evening	30.00
Vedanta : The Supreme Knowledge	30.00
Vedanta : An Art of Dying	30.00
A Teste of the Divine	30.00
One Earth One Humanity	30.00
Freedom from the Mind	30.00
Life A Song, A Dance	30.00
Meeting the Ultimate	30.00
The Master is a Mirror	30.00
Rishing in Love	30.00
The Forgotten Language of the Heart	30.00
The Alchemy of Enlightenment	30.00
From Ignorance to Innocence	30.00
Be Silent & Know	30.00
Turning In Tantra Vision : The Secret of The Inner Experience	30.00
Tantra Vision : An Invitation of Silence	30.00
Tantra Vision : Beyond the Barriers of Wisdom	30.00
Tantra Vision : The Door to Nirvana	30.00
Eternal Celebration	30.00
A Song Without Words	30.00
Inner Harmony	30.00
Sing, Dance, Rejoice	30.00
Secret of Disciplehood	30.00
Laughter s my message	30.00
The Mystery Beyond Mind	30.00
The Centre of the Cyclone	30.00
Meditation : The Ultimate Adventure	30.00
The Cessation of Mind	30.00
The Birth of Being	30.00
Love & Medition	30.00
I Say unto you (Vol. I)	120.00
I Say unto you (Vol. II)	120.00
Divine Melody	80.00
A Cup of Tea	120.00

STORY BOOKS NOVEL

Mansarovar-I	Munshi Prem Chand	95.00
Toote Kante	Dr. Vrindavan Lal Verma	60.00
Savera (Novel) The Morning	Joginder Singh Karwal	20.00
Kamayani (Jaishanker Prasad)	B. K. Chaturvedi	50.00
Aansoo	Jaishanker Prasad	15.00
In The Shadows of Taj (Noval)	Amita Sahaya	40.00

Diamond Pocket Books (P) Ltd. X-30, Okhla Industrial Area, Phase-II, New Delhi-110020

डायमंड पॉकेट बुक्स (प्रा.) लि.
धार्मिक व पूजा पाठ की अनुपम पुस्तकें

मर्यादा पुरुषोत्तम भगवान राम*	काली उपासना
दिव्य आभा मण्डल (Aura)*	विष्णु उपासना
प्रज्ञावेणु (गीता व्याख्या) मुक्त छन्द में*	गणेश उपासना
मानस प्रेमसूत्र-I, II(मुरारी बापू)*	सरस्वती उपासना
मानस भुसुण्डी गीता(मुरारी बापू)*	ऋग्वेद (सरल भाषा में)*
रामचरितामृत*	सामवेद (सरल भाषा में)*
आरती संग्रह	यजुर्वेद (सरल भाषा में)*
गजानन (जीवनी)	अर्थववेद (सरल भाषा में)*
वेदान्त दर्शन	108 उपनिषद*
मीमांसा दर्शन	सुख सागर*
सांख्य दर्शन	प्रभु मिलन का मार्ग
युग प्रवर्तक गौतम बुद्ध	जैकारा शेरांवली का
कार्तिक महात्मय*	व्रत पर्व और त्यौहार
मनुस्मृति*	रामायण*
विदुर नीति*	बाल्मीकि रामायण
भर्तृहरि शतक	महाभारत*
अनेकता में एकता	सिक्खों के दस गुरु*
नवीन रामलीला नाटक*	श्रीमद् भागवत् गीता*
गणेश पुराण	शिरडी के साईं बाबा*
भविष्य पुराण	कथा सरित सागर*
पद्म पुराण	योग वशिष्ठ*
वराह पुराण	दशावतार
कूर्म पुराण	चाणक्य नीति*
ब्रह्म पुराण	चाणक्य सूत्र*
माकण्डेय पुराण	कौटिल्य अर्थशास्त्र
मत्स्य पुराण	आर्य पुष्पांजलि
ब्रह्माण्ड पुराण	गुरु वशिष्ठ
श्री विष्णु पुराण	दुर्गा सप्तशती
श्री शिव पुराण	नीलकंठ
श्री देवी भागवत पुराण	प्रजापति, ब्रह्म
ब्रह्मवैवर्त पुराण	भगवान परशुराम
गायत्री उपासना	सत्य साई बाबा*
लक्ष्मी उपासना	श्रीमद भगवत गीता(आधुनिक व्याख्या)

डायमंड पॉकेट बुक्स (प्रा.) लि.
X-30, ओखला इन्डस्ट्रियल एरिया, फेज़—2, नई दिल्ली—110020

DIAMOND POCKET BOOKS
NEW PUBLICATION

Yoga For Better Health	Acharya Bhagwan Dev	40.00
Ladies Health Guide (With Make-Up Guide)	Usha Rai Verma	75.00
Skin Care	Dr. Renu Gupta	60.00
Brilliant Light (Reiki Grand Master Manual)	M. Subramaniam	195.00
Ayurvedic Cure For Common Diseases	Acharya Vipul Rao	75.00
Low Calories Diet	Tehlina Kaul	95.00
Common Diseases of Women	Dr. Renu Gupta.	75.00
Diseases of Respiratory Tract Causes & Cure of Heart Ailments	Dr. Satish Goel	60.00
Surya Chikitsa	Acharya Satyanand	60.00
Causes and Cure of Stress (Migraine & Headache)	Dr. Shiv Kumar	75.00
Acupressure Guide	Dr. Satish Goel	40.00
Acupuncture Guide	Dr. Satish Goel	40.00
Joys of Parenthood	Dr. R. N. Gupta	40.00
Tips on Sex	Dr. S. K. Sharma	75.00
Herbs That Heal	Acharya Vipul Rao	75.00
Causes, Cure and Prevention of Nervous Diseases	Dr. Shiv Kumar	75.00
Cheiro's Language of The Hand	Cheiro	40.00
Cheiro's Book of Astrology	Cheiro	50.00
Cheiro's Book of Numberology	Cheiro	30.00
Children Jokes	G.C.Goel (Editor)	40.00
Delighting Jokes	G.C.Goel (Editor)	40.00
Thrilling Jokes	G. C. Goel (Editor)	40.00
Hilarious Jokes	G. C. Goel (Editor)	40.00
Kautilya Arthshastra	B.K. Chaturvedi	25.00
Clinton Lewinsky Scandal	Ashok Kumar Sharma	60,00
Jyotish & Santan Yog	Dr. Bhojraj Dwivedi	75.00
Sensational Sachin	Lokesh Thani	60.00
Super Star Ajay Jadeja	Lokesh Thani	40.00
English-English Hindi Dictionary	Dr. Baljit Singh & Dr. Giriraj Sharan Agarwal	150.00
Songs of Rafi		30.00
Hit Songs of Lata		30.00
Hit Songs of Kishore		30.00
Hit Songs of Mukesh		30.00

DIAMOND POCKET BOOKS (P) LTD.
X-30, Okhla Industrial Area, Phase-II, New Delhi-110020